MIRACLES
ARE
CONTAGIOUS!

Praise for *The Miracles in You*

"*The Miracles in You* is a very special book that will help you have a miracle mindset, see the miracles around you, and experience them in you. If you need a miracle or just want them elevated in your life, read and live this book."

Daniel Amen, MD, author of *Change Your Brain, Change Your Life*

"A miracle-creating mindset begins when you inundate your conscious mind with the idea that you can create miracles. Then the subconscious comes into alignment with that idea, and executes it flawlessly. In *The Miracles in You,* Mark Victor Hansen inspires us all to open ourselves to receiving and creating miracles . . . and in the process creating an intentional wave of goodness across the world."

Sharon Lechter, CPA CGMA, author of *Think and Grow Rich for Women,*
and coauthor of *Outwitting the Devil,*
Three Feet from Gold, and *Rich Dad Poor Dad*

"Miracles are mesmerizing to the human soul. My friend Mark Victor Hansen clearly teaches how you can experience and create more miracles than you ever imagined."

Peter Guber, chairman and CEO of Mandalay Entertainment,
best-selling author of *Tell to Win*, and owner of the
Los Angeles Dodgers and Golden State Warriors

"Many people do not believe in miracles. Both Mark Victor Hansen and I have experienced or witnessed many miracles. His descriptions of these events in this book will help all readers, including skeptics, believe in those inexplicable, intangible aspects of humanity."

Benjamin S. Carson Sr., MD, emeritus professor of neurosurgery,
oncology, plastic surgery, and pediatrics at Johns Hopkins Medicine
and president and CEO of American Business Collaborative, LLC

"*The Miracles in You* gives straight talk on miracles from a proven winner. Mark Victor Hansen shows why he is the # 1 author on the planet for good reason. His story is a miracle and his new book inspires me to realize all of us are as well. It is refreshing to read something that fosters positive thinking and self-assuredness that have long been the hallmarks of Mark's work and our country's greatness. It is an inspiration to all and a pleasure to read."

Ronald Bloomingkemper, Chairman of Freedom Equity Group

"My wife and I just finished reading *The Miracles in You*, and I have to agree with her statement, 'That was one of the best books I have ever read!' For generations, the common worldview of miracles has been quite similar to a dimly lit stage full of black and white cardboard characters. Through Mark's book, God breathed the breath of life into the cardboard characters, making them real again and revealing the fact that the animated performers are you and me, and that miracles are the tapestry God has woven into our every day lives—we need only to observe and recognize this truth. I believe this book will start a chain reaction of great miracles that cannot be stopped."

Dr. Mick Hall, developer of the "35 For Life" program

"*The Miracles in You* is the Mark Victor Hansen I know and love. Like all great leaders, he sweeps us off our feet, promising and delivering personal life experiences we never thought possible. Mark makes waking up exciting and shows how living with character and purpose is an honor. At a time in our lives when shock and horror fill the 24-hour news, I pray that another soul is touched by this wonderful book."

David J. D'Arcangelo, president of the D'Arcangelo Companies
and author of *The Secret Asset*

"I'm a big fan of God and of Mark Victor Hansen. If you read *The Miracles in You*, they will both help you open your life to the possibility of receiving and creating miracles. A fabulous read!"

Ken Blanchard, coauthor of *The One Minute Manager*® and *Lead Like Jesus*

THE
MIRACLES
IN YOU

RECOGNIZING GOD'S AMAZING WORK
IN YOU AND THROUGH YOU

Mark Victor Hansen

WORTHY®
PUBLISHING

Published by Worthy Books, an imprint of Worthy Publishing Group, a division of Worthy Media, Inc., 134 Franklin Road, Suite 200, Brentwood, Tennessee 37027.

WORTHY is a registered trademark of Worthy Media, Inc.

HELPING PEOPLE EXPERIENCE THE HEART OF GOD

eBook available wherever digital books are sold.

Library of Congress Control Number: 2015931432

For foreign and subsidiary rights, contact rights@worthypublishing.com

Published in association with Ted Squires Agency, Nashville, Tennessee

ISBN: 978-1-61795-482-5
ISBN: 978-1-61795-902-8 (Spanish edition)

Cover Design: Christopher Tobias, Tobias' Outerwear for Books
Interior Design and Typesetting: Bart Dawson

Printed in the United States of America

15 16 17 18 19 VPI 8 7 6 5 4 3 2 1

I dedicate this book to

YOU!

The flame of your miracle-generating candle

can light

one,

a hundred,

a thousand,

or even millions more.

Be a light.

Be a miracle generator!

CONTENTS

Foreword

by Dr. Ben Carson

Whether or not one believes in miracles is immaterial. They occur whether you acknowledge them or not. Sometimes it is necessary to be both vigilant and introspective to recognize the miracles in our lives. I have witnessed many miracles, but I would like to highlight one in particular.

When I was a young teenager, I had a particularly violent temper. It was not unusual for me to go after people with bricks and sticks and baseball bats. I even tried to hit my own mother in the head with a hammer during a fit of rage. Fortunately, my brother caught the hammer from behind and was able to restrain me.

One fateful day, I had a large camping knife on my person when another teenager angered me. I lunged at him with the knife, trying to stab him in the abdomen. Fortunately, a large metal belt buckle under his clothing took the brunt of the force and actually caused the knife blade to break. He fled in terror, but I was even more horrified as I recognized that I was trying to kill someone over nothing. I locked myself in the bathroom and tearfully contemplated my circumstances. I recognized that had that belt buckle not been in place, my friend would have been seriously injured or killed, and my dream of becoming a physician would have been dealt a deathblow.

I am convinced until this day that God worked a miracle in my life to affect such a dramatic change almost instantaneously. The resulting calmness and steadiness were instrumental in my successful career as a neurosurgeon and in my post-retirement foray into the political world.

I fell to my knees and implored God to help me with this temper problem. There was a Bible in the bathroom, and I picked it up and turned it to the book of Proverbs and began to read. There were so many verses about fools and about anger, and it seemed as if they were all written about me. I remained in the bathroom for three hours reading, praying, and contemplating my life. I came to a miraculous understanding that to react angrily and try to hurt others was actually a sign of weakness and selfishness. That was the very last day of my life that I had an angry outburst. I am convinced until this day that God worked a miracle in my life to affect such a dramatic change almost instantaneously. The resulting calmness and steadiness were instrumental in my successful career as a neurosurgeon and in my post-retirement foray into the political world.

Some have claimed that my transformation reflects my ability to conceal my anger. That would mean the change was really only a paint job; in fact, it was a change of heart, and the anger is simply no longer there. Such a change can only be explained by the intervention of a power greater than ourselves. Is that not what a miracle is?

I hope you will enjoy this tome by Mark Victor Hansen, which is based on many true stories about miracles that have had life-changing outcomes for many people, some of whom are quite well-known.

Introduction

Most people have a "wait and see" view of miracles. They may believe that miracles happen, but they don't know when, how, or why they will. They simply sit. And they wait. And they pray. They believe miracles *only* come in the supernatural, fire-in-the-sky explosions of God's divine intervention. And some believe miracles *only* happened in the past. They're wrong.

While there is no doubt that mankind has received many heavenly gifts of supernatural origin—seen all through Scripture and even in your local newspaper if you know how to look—there are also other kinds of miracles. These miracles happen many times a day, to or around every single one of us, all over the world. These miracles are simple actions or words that enter our lives and change them for the better. These interactions may seem plain and ordinary at first, but over time you can see how they completely change the trajectory of your life. They create results that could never have been achieved without "miraculous" intervention. These are the miracles *we* can create. God has placed these miracles within each of us, waiting to be released.

What would happen if seven billion people each created just one miracle? Perhaps this book will inspire many of them. That is certainly my hope and prayer.

Making Miracles

Jesus is, without question, the ultimate Miracle Maker. Even those who don't normally read the Bible cannot escape the power of His miracle stories in Scripture. In my reading of the gospels, I count thirty-seven different times when Jesus worked a miracle. There were healings, exorcisms, and displays of supernatural knowledge. He even turned water into wine and raised a man from the dead! Surely, everyone who came into contact with Jesus felt His miracle-making power and potential. I wonder how many more miracles Jesus created that aren't recorded in Scripture. I wonder how many of His seemingly insignificant interactions with people resulted in the quiet miracles that went somewhat unnoticed but resulted in changing someone's life forever. Maybe that's what the apostle John is referring to in the closing passage of his gospel: "Jesus did many other things as well. If every one of them were written down, I suppose that even the whole world would not have room for the books that would be written" (John 21:25).

There are no limits on miracles, yet most people live as though they're not entitled to any. They act like miracles are performed by and happen to other people but never them. Not so! Jesus boldly states in John 14:12, "Very truly I tell you, whoever believes in me will do the works [miracles] I have been doing, and they will do even greater things than these, because I am going to the Father." Does that seem impossible? It's not.

There are no limits on miracles, yet most people live as though they're not entitled to any. They act like miracles are performed by and happen to other people but never them. Not so!

I've seen the evidence of God's miracles, great and small, throughout the course of my life. I could look back on almost any day of my life and show you a string of miracles that God accomplished for me *and* those that He enabled me to do for other people. No, I've never raised anyone from the dead, but I *have* helped save someone's life. I didn't create the earth, but I *did* help save a nation. There was a time when I thought these things were good fortune or coincidence, but now I know better. Now I know that God has used me to do a lot of miracles in the world. That may sound like bragging, but nothing could be further from the truth. It's not bragging to praise God for the way He's worked in my life and in others' lives to do such amazing things. In fact, it's incredibly humbling to realize that He is not only *willing* to use me at all, but that He *chooses* to work through me so often!

The Miracle Journey

Miracles may sometimes appear to be spontaneous, but that doesn't mean they're accidental. Every miracle is the result of an intentional act or decision, whether it's a direct act of God or a more "common" miracle that God allows us to perform. In order to unlock our full miracle-making potential, we need to be intentional about walking through a progression that I call the Miracle Journey.

The first step is to *Believe the Miracle*. My friend, miracles exist. They are real. They are not coincidences. They are not "happy accidents." They are planned, intentional acts of God to show off His power and His love, and to make this world a better place. But there are so many more miracles in the world than the wondrous ones recorded in the Bible! As we get started on the Miracle Journey, we first need to broaden our view of what miracles are so we can better position ourselves to see them in our lives and the lives of others.

The second step is to *See the Miracle*. God is at work in your life, and He has been all along. He's stepped in supernaturally and changed the course of your life many times. And, of course, He's used other people in your life to continually guide, bless, and instruct you all along. On our way to becoming miracle makers, we first have to stop and recognize all the amazing miracles in our own lives.

Miracles don't happen by accident. God can and will step in at any moment and use you to bless someone, but that doesn't mean you can't *also* look for ways to bless them too.

The third step is to *Be the Miracle*. Now we're cooking! Remember, miracles don't happen by accident. God can and will step in at any moment and use you to bless someone, but that doesn't mean you can't *also* look for ways to bless them too. Once you recognize that miracles exist and you start to see how God has moved mountains in your own life, you'll develop an insatiable hunger to be that catalyst in the life of someone else. It creates an indescribable feeling of unity and cooperation with God, and it is truly one of the most thrilling feelings you'll ever experience.

Miracle Scrolls

Throughout the book, following the chapters, I will share with you different inspirational statements I call *Miracle Scrolls*. I want you to take them into your spirit. Bookmark them. Read at least one a day, before you rise in the morning or just before you close your eyes at night. These Miracle Scrolls will serve to bring your mind to full awareness of your magnificent miracle-making potential.

To become a miracle worker, you just have to decide you can be one! And when you decide, God will provide. God will fill your heart with what you need for every unique endeavor. When you believe and activate miracles, you are saying yes to your destiny, and to the purpose for which you were created. Please don't settle for anything less.

A Miraculous Life

As I write this I am in Macau, on the East China Sea, look-ing out over the beautiful waters. I am feeling enormously blessed. I have married my twin flame, my ultimate soul mate. I have an amazing circle of dear friends and family. My work is my passion. As I take all of this in, I realize how extraordi-nary my life has been—nothing short of miraculous! As my wife, Crystal, and I take a few days rest from our book tour in China, I've been thinking about all the twists and turns and amazing events I've experienced. The great things. The things that seemed bad at the time but often turned out to be good. The things that seemed bad and stayed bad. Yet all these things opened the doors to one miracle after another. The next was always greater than the last!

Throughout this book, you will meet people who "dreamed the impossible dream." They believed, took action, and changed the world for the better. I promise that at least one of these stories will move your heart, mind, and soul. I promise that you will find your own life opening up to the possibility of receiving *and creating* a miracle—and perhaps many more than one.

Although I don't know your spiritual disposition at the moment, I believe that God has put His hand on my shoulder and told me to write this book for you. My wish is to uplift your spirit, mind, heart, and soul. As you read these pages, I pray that you will discover miracle-making power in you that you never noticed before. My mission is for you to see and accept this power, and to believe it at the deepest level of your soul.

Now, it's my hope and belief that your life will be one miracle after another. It is your divine right and, I believe, your destiny. That is why you are reading this book. Journey with me now, and let's move forward to discover the miracles inside of you!

PART I

Believe
the Miracle

1

Miracles Are Everywhere

D o you want to hear about a genuine miracle?"

The question took me completely off guard. My wife and I had stopped at the store to pick up a few things, and I had struck up a conversation with the cashier at the counter. I'd spent the last few months working on this very book, so as soon as he said the word *miracle*, he had my complete attention.

"Absolutely!" was my reply. "Tell me all about it."

This young man went on to tell me in vivid detail about his wife's recent near-death experience. She was driving down a busy street when suddenly, she realized her car had no brakes! She was cruising along, with cars and pedestrians all around, but she was completely unable to stop—or even slow—her speeding car. Purely by instinct, she began to pray, *Please, God, protect me. Stop this car. Keep me from hitting another car. Get all of these pedestrians out of the way. Get us all home safe.* After several terrifying seconds, the car had come to a hard stop thanks to the tree that was now firmly planted in her front bumper. Somehow, her car had made it through the maze of traffic and passers-by without incident. The car was wrecked, but everyone, including my new friend's wife, went home safe that night. "It was a miracle," the cashier repeated.

I thought about that for a second and asked him, "So, how do you think that miracle happened?"

His response could not have been more perfect in light of all the miracle stories I had been studying while working on this book: "We're all prayed up, brother. We're all prayed up, and we *always* have miracles."

I love that answer. "We're all prayed up, and we *always* have miracles." That young man had no idea that by simply telling me that story, he was actually *making* a miracle. He didn't know who I was. He didn't know that I'd written several best-selling books or that I was currently writing one about miracles. He just felt inspired to tell his story, and in doing so God worked through him to remind me that He was there with me as I wrote this book. God was reminding me that miracles are everywhere.

Now, you may read this and say, "Mark, you're making that story up. That's the kind of story preachers and writers tell just to get a point across." No, this conversation *did indeed* happen. Of course it happened. Why wouldn't it happen? Why should we be surprised when we find ourselves standing in the middle of an experience that could only be described as miraculous? Why shouldn't we hear stories like that day after day after day?

His response could not have been more perfect in light of all the miracle stories I had been studying while working on this book: "We're all prayed up, brother. We're all prayed up, and we *always* have miracles."

Miracles are all around us. Sometimes it's God miraculously moving the immovable obstacles in our lives. Sometimes it's a miraculous healing from a terminal diagnosis. Sometimes, as with this cashier's wife, it is moving people and cars out of the way and putting a tree in the perfect spot to stop an out-of-control car. Those are the kinds of things where we have no choice but to look up to the heavens and say, "God, You did this. There's no other explanation."

But there are other miracles that all too often go unnoticed. These are the miracles that are walking and talking all around us. They sit in the cubicles next to us at work. They share the subway or airplane with us. They're around us in movie theaters or at church. They're in the cars next to us on the interstate, or in line beside us at baseball games, or even behind the counter at the local market. You, everyone you know, and everyone you ever come into contact with have the potential to become miracle makers. And when you embrace the truth that God works miracles through normal men and women every single day, you not only begin to *notice* the miracles around you; you begin to *become* the miracle in someone else's life.

The Miracle Mindset

Albert Einstein once said, "Either everything is a miracle or nothing is a miracle." I try to be miracle minded at all times, so naturally I fall more on the "everything is a miracle" side of things. That miracle mindset changes how you view the world. When you inundate your mind and spirit with the belief that God wants to work miracles in you and through you, your whole being—your mind, body, spirit, and subconscious—comes into alignment and sets the course of your life on a miracle-making trajectory. That's certainly been true in my life.

In 1974, I was a bankrupt twenty-six-year-old former millionaire. I was crushed. I was so low that year that I had to reach up to touch bottom. To be honest, I think it was a miracle that I made it through that year alive.

Around that time, someone gave me an inspirational audio program by Cavett Robert, the Dean of Speakers and co-founder of the National Speakers Association. The audio was titled *Are You the Cause or Are You the Result?* In that life-changing presentation, Cavett struck me with one of the most powerful truths of my life: "Either you are the creature of circumstances or the creator of circumstances. You cannot be both." That message cut me to the core. It was as though Cavett was speaking directly into my despair, asking if I wanted to be a victim or a leader. Did I want to be someone whom things *happened to*, or did I want to be someone who *made things happen*?

Over the course of the next several weeks and months, I kept a record of how many times I listened to that audio program, like a western gunslinger putting notches on his pistol. I listened to that message 287 times. I knew in my heart that Cavett was feeding my soul and reprogramming my misguided mind.

One morning, as God was putting my life and mind back together, I woke up with a start. Out of the blue, I knew without a doubt what God's destiny for my life was. I had a vision for where He was taking me. I came through that dark time in my life with a clear goal: become a professional speaker and author. From that point on, my mind was fixated on that goal.

At the time, I was sharing a rental house with four other guys. Over breakfast one day, I asked them if anyone knew any professional speakers whom I could talk to about how to get started. My roommate John said, "There's a dynamic young guy named Chip Collins talking this morning to all my real estate colleagues." It was 8:30 a.m. when I heard this announcement. Less than thirty minutes later I was taking my seat in the real estate group, ready to experience Chip wow the crowd for the next three hours.

I took Chip to lunch after his presentation and asked if he

could help me get started in the world of professional speaking. He agreed, as long I stayed out of his market. He thought I'd have better luck targeting what he called "the bottomless pit of motivational training needed in the life insurance business." He told me that day that I had a one-in-a-thousand chance of succeeding, but to do whatever I could over the next two weeks while he was out of town. He said, "The chances of you making it are very low, but if you do, I'll see you when I get back."

Two weeks later, Chip got back into town—and I had twenty-eight paying clients in the life insurance industry for my new speaking business. I was already doing four one-hour talks a day, and I spent the hours in between running around town trying to drum up more business. I was speaking for a living, and I was in heaven. Of course, I had no real experience in speaking or training, and I certainly didn't know anything about the life insurance business. I couldn't tell the difference between term and whole life. I didn't know what a premium was. I didn't even *own* life insurance at the time, but here I was spending all day every day providing life training and motivation to rooms full of insurance professionals!

You see, the one thing I had was the one thing that mattered most: desire. I had a white-hot desire to learn and master the fine art of speaking, training, and writing. It was my magnificent obsession. It was my miracle mindset.

As I focused more and more on the call God put in my life, and as I trusted Him to move the mountains out of my path, miracle after miracle paved my way. It was a miracle that I met Chip Collins and that he was willing to coach me in my new enterprise. It was a miracle that one of my very first clients was the most influential and successful leader in his company, and that he got me in the door with more willing prospects than I could have dreamed of. It was a miracle that I was paid for more than five hundred talks in that first year. It was a miracle that every one of those clients invested in me by either educating me on the insurance industry or introducing me to new prospects.

God is actively moving in your life. He is doing wondrous things, not only in the supernatural realm, but also in the day-to-day interactions you have with other people.

I was living in the flood of God's provision and miracles, and I loved every minute of it. I was reminded of the apostle

Paul's words to the Ephesians, "Now to him who is able to do immeasurably more than all we ask or imagine, according to his power that is at work within us, to him be glory in the church and in Christ Jesus throughout all generations, for ever and ever!" (Ephesians 3:20-21). God was indeed doing immeasurably more than I could ask or imagine, because His power was at work within me—just as it is within you. Fully grasping that truth—truly embracing the miracle mindset—changes everything.

Your Miraculous Story

I'm telling you this part of my story for one reason, and that is to convince you that we must never underestimate the power of our stories. They have the potential to change the world. How do I know? Well, collecting powerful stories has been my passion for decades. Years ago Jack Canfield and I created the Chicken Soup for the Soul series, and since the first book released, thousands of people have felt compelled to tell me their stories. I've heard incredible stories of how God used our little books to change people's minds about suicide, to change the direction of the whole nation of Lebanon, to seek out adventure in foreign lands, to start a new enterprise, to find the perfect spouse, and so much more. It is unbelievably humbling to see what God has done simply because we have helped people tell their stories.

So, as you go through this book, I want to encourage you to think about your own miraculous story. Later, we'll spend several chapters examining how to *see the miracle*, or trace God's miraculous provision through your life as you seek ways to *be the miracle*. But for now, I want to ask you to simply *believe the miracle*. God is actively moving in your life. He is doing wondrous things, not only in the supernatural realm, but also in the day-to-day interactions you have with other people. Even something as simple as a smile from a stranger or a helping hand from a neighbor could be the evidence of the Creator of the universe coming alongside you and moving you forward.

If that seems like an impossibility to you, I ask only that for the next thirty days you believe that miracles are possible for you. And if you believe that, even if it's only because I'm asking you to, then spend time each evening reflecting on how God may have touched your life that day. Take notes. Pay attention to the "random acts of kindness" you see. Open your eyes to what God may be doing in you, through you, and around you. That is how you develop the miracle mind-set, and that's how you start to develop your own miraculous story.

First Miracle Scroll

Miracles Are Natural for Me

God wants my life to be full of miracles.

My life itself is a miracle.

Miracles are happening to me continuously.

I wake daily and experience the miracle of living.

My miracles are expanding and accelerating.

I think about miracles, so they come about.

My dreams are miraculous because

I program myself to them before I sleep,

expecting, thinking, and feeling the joy of miracles.

Upon arising I give myself this affirmation:

Today I expect and happily receive miracles.

2

Understanding Miracles

D o you believe in miracles? YES!" cried the thirty-five-year-old sports announcer Al Michaels as the crowd counted down the last five seconds of what *Sports Illustrated* named the top sports moment of the 20th Century during it's *20th Century Sports Awards* show in December 1999. The moment, of course, was the U.S. Olympic hockey team's defeat of the Soviet Union in the 1980 Winter Olympics, a game that immediately became known as, fittingly enough, The Miracle on Ice.

The Soviets came into the games with nothing but

confidence. Their team was comprised of professional play-ers and even some active-duty soldiers. They had access to world-class training facilities. They had won the gold medal in six of the previous seven Olympic games. In all of their Olympic matches going back twenty years, the Soviet team had won twenty-seven out of twenty-nine games, with one tie and only one loss.

In contrast, the American team was made up of college players and amateurs. Only one of the twenty members of the U.S. Olympic team had played in the games before. The team was young too—the youngest team in U.S. Olympic history and the youngest team to play in the 1980 games at all. Several of the teammates were former rivals from their respective college teams. Just two weeks before the American victory on February 22, 1980, the Soviet team demolished Team U.S.A. 10–3 in an exhibition game.

All of this led *New York Times* columnist Dave Anderson to write a hopeless appraisal just one day before the U.S.-Soviet matchup: "Unless the ice melts, or unless the United States team or another team performs a miracle . . . the Russians are expected to easily win the Olympic gold medal."[1] There's that word again: *miracle*.

Well, you probably know the end of the story. The U.S.

team did, in fact, perform a miracle. With ten minutes left on the clock, Team U.S.A. took a 4–3 lead and held on to it for ten long, tense minutes. The crowd was at such a fever pitch that all 8,500 spectators screamed the countdown in the final ten seconds. With five seconds left on the clock, when it was clear that the Americans had secured the victory, sportscaster Al Michaels simply couldn't contain himself any longer. He cried out his now-famous words.

Do you believe in miracles?

YES!

Yes, I believe in miracles. I believe that God does amazing, supernatural acts of beauty and wonder. And yes, I believe that a team of hard-working, idealistic young adults can do miracles too. Isn't it interesting that the whole world immediately made the connection between a simple hockey game and one of the most powerful words in the English language? There was even a movie made about this story. When the producers and studio executives were considering titles, they settled on one single, all-encompassing, all-inspiring word: *Miracle*. Why? Because they knew how powerful the word was, and because they knew moviegoers—and the rest of us—long to be reminded of the presence of miracles in our lives.

What Is a Miracle?

As I have heard literally thousands of miracle stories from people all over the world, and as I have matured in my own faith journey, I've faced all the questions you no doubt have yourself:

> *What is a miracle?*
> *Do miracles really exist?*
> *Are miracles something that happened only in the Bible?*
> *Are miracles wholly divine intervention?*
> *Or do some miracles start out with God and then find completion through us?*

Such great questions! And they contain traces of the tension between the human element and the divine element. Culture and Scripture each view the miracle question a bit differently, so let's look at both for just a minute.

The Bible never outright defines what it means by "miracle." However, if you consider some of the more common miracle tales in Scripture—Moses parting the Red Sea or Jesus raising Lazarus from the dead, for example—you can see a common theme. The term *miracle* there refers to a supernatural act by which God, the Creator of the natural world, intervenes and temporarily alters the natural order He established. If you don't believe that an intelligent Creator brought the universe into existence, then you can't believe in this type of miracle. After all, if the natural laws are pre-existent and have no Creator, then there is no force that can interrupt them. However, if you believe there is a God with the power to *make* mountains, then you must necessarily believe He also has the power to *move* mountains, right? And that is how God acts supernaturally in the world, stepping in and, for the benefit of His children, altering the natural order of things in specific instances.

If you believe there is a God with the power to *make* mountains, then you must necessarily believe He also has the power to *move* mountains, right? And that is how God acts supernaturally in the world.

Of course, that's not necessarily how culture defines the term. We use the word *miracle* to refer to almost any situation that is a combination of happy, exciting, surprising, and unexpected. That's why the word *miracle* was universally applied to a specific hockey game. If you see the word *miracle* in Scripture, someone likely just walked on water or was healed from leprosy. If you hear it out on the street today, it may just mean that someone got a good parking spot. There seems to be a wide gap between the biblical view and our cultural view, but I'm not convinced it's a gap at all. Why couldn't God bless us with a good parking spot? If we're stuck on the side of a seemingly abandoned road and a friendly passerby appears out of nowhere to help us change a flat tire, why couldn't that be God working through someone to bring blessing into our lives?

After all, Scripture clearly states, "Every good and perfect gift is from above, coming down from the Father of the heavenly lights, who does not change like shifting shadows" (James 1:17). Jesus Himself declared, "If you, then, though you are evil, know how to give good gifts to your children, how much more will your Father in heaven give good gifts to those who ask him" (Matthew 7:11). These passages fill me with warmth, because they show me that there is an almighty Father who knows me, who loves me, and who actively showers His blessings upon me. That assurance, combined with a miracle mindset, enables me to see God's work in and through my life in a million different ways! He can move mountains to bless me—and He has. Or He could reach out in the hand of a friend—and He certainly has done this too.

I am convinced there is a first cause, God, and that He often chooses to work miracles through second causes (other people). And if I believe that, then I have to believe that He wants to use me to become a "second cause" for others.

I like this definition of the word *miracle,* found in *Easton's Bible Dictionary* as well as other sources:

The simple and grand truth that the universe is not under the exclusive control of physical forces, but that everywhere and always there is above, separate from and superior to all else, an infinite personal will, not superseding, but directing and controlling all physical causes, acting with or without them. God ordinarily effects his purpose through the agency of second causes; but he has the power also of effecting his purpose immediately and without the intervention of second causes, i.e., of invading the fixed order, and thus of working miracles. Thus we affirm the possibility of miracles, the possibility of a higher hand intervening to control or reverse nature's ordinary movements.

I am convinced there is a first cause, God, and that He often chooses to work miracles through second causes (other people). And if I believe that, then I have to believe that He wants to use me to become a "second cause" for others. That's how He uses me to make miracles.

Miracles of Innovation

The eighteenth-century French philosopher Voltaire said, "If you mean by miracle an effect of which you cannot perceive the cause, in that sense all is miracle." Actually, there is a clear progression from the unknown to the known that I teach in my seminars. First comes fiction; then comes the theoretical understanding of the real principles underlying the fiction; and finally there is the physical manifestation of what used to be seen as mere fantasy. The miracles we get to participate in always start as ideas, beliefs, hopes, dreams, speeches, discussions, mastermind sessions, visions, concepts, innovations, or even as problems.

In 1875, all the newspapers in America were in a panic about how the country was running out of whale oil. Two partners, John D. Rockefeller and Henry M. Flagler, figured out how to build a better and more cost-effective oil refinery. The timing and innovation each was, dare I say, a miracle! The first gasoline-powered automobile debuted just eleven years later, which sparked the explosive growth of the auto industry, complete with thousands of new cars in precious need of oil and gasoline. That, plus the invention and rapid growth of airplanes in the early twentieth century, miraculously transformed Rockefeller's small, chaotic oil business into a trillion-dollar industry that literally powers the world as we know it.

Several years ago, I had the honor of sharing the stage with another visionary, Jay Walker. Jay is America's best-known business inventor and entrepreneur. When I met him, he had just been on the cover of *Forbes* magazine, which called him the next Thomas Edison. Jay is a master at giving flesh to ideas. He has created massive, world-changing businesses out of what some people would call thin air. He was awarded the first Invisible Patent for his creation of priceline.com, a service that found a way to sell the empty seats on flights just before takeoff for a great value. It was a win-win for Priceline and for the airlines, because it turned non-revenue-creating seats into a huge source of profit for both. That's what Jay does; he turns ideas into real, nuts-and-bolts businesses. Jay now has over 719 utility patents and has the distinction of being the eleventh most-patented person alive. Jay Walker is an idea man, and because of that, he's also a miracle man.

Jules Verne is perhaps one of my very favorite miracle-creating visionaries. He built big ideas into his novels in the nineteenth century. Practically everything he imagined would have been considered a miracle at the time if they had existed. Verne wrote about "preposterous" things, such as manned aircraft, deep-sea underwater explorations, and men landing on the moon. These were all impossible dreams that, perhaps because Jules Verne implanted the ideas into the collective consciousness of the world, somehow became reality within the following hundred and fifty years.

These are all examples of what I call "miracles of innovation." They started with a simple idea and passion, and the results were inventions or industries that literally changed the world. Now, are these things genuine miracles? Yes! Remember, God can choose to use "second causes" to do mighty things in the world. He could have created an airplane out of nothing and dropped it in the Garden of Eden with Adam and Eve, but instead He chose to inspire men to bring that wonderful creation into the world. Just because it was dreamed up by human minds and built by human hands doesn't mean it isn't a miracle. I believe we are truly at our best when we are working in cooperation with the Creator, allowing Him to work in and through us to bring new and amazing things into the world. That may result in changing the course of history, or it may simply change the course of someone's day. When we're in that constant state of cooperation with God, when we allow that miracle mindset to guide our actions, the miracles will come in all shapes and sizes—but all are significant.

Second Miracle Scroll

I Am One of God's Greatest Miracles

I am one of God's greatest miracles.

God made me in His image and likeness (Genesis 1:27).

God created the heavens and the earth.

God created me to create.

I am free to create miracles.

Many of the men and women in the Bible

created miracles.

The Source of miracles is the same yesterday,

today, and forever.

Miracles are my inheritance and destiny.

God's destiny for me is to create miracles.

I am and will always be one of

God's greatest miracles.

3

God Makes Miracles

What must the Israelites have been thinking? Can you imagine what was going through their minds as they watched the waters of the great Red Sea—a seemingly impassable obstacle—rise up into the air to reveal a dry path of land? This is one of the most well-known stories in the entire Bible. Whether you were raised in church or not, you have no doubt heard this story countless times going back to your earliest memories or seen the event depicted in movies or art.

God's parting the waters has become an iconic image, one that almost everyone has heard about. And, honestly, that kind of exposure may be a problem. You see, when a miracle of such magnitude gets that kind of exposure for so long, we start to lose sight of the awe and wonder of it all. It's as though the story itself has become a caricature of the miraculous, and that is tragic.

The power that parted the Red Sea is the same power that works in the world today. It's the same power that works miracles in us and through us, no matter how significant (or insignificant) they appear at the time.

I've spent time in the biggest cities in the world, walking down some of the busiest sidewalks. I've looked up from those sidewalks more times than I can count to admire the enormous buildings to my right and left. I've been awestruck at what it must have taken to build such incredible towers that from a street-level perspective seem to reach all the way to the clouds. Maybe you can picture that: standing on a crowded New York City sidewalk with some of the tallest buildings in the world on either side. Now, just for a moment, imagine that those intimidating walls were not made of stone, concrete, and glass—but of water. Rather than looking through windows and seeing people moving about inside, you see schools of fish swimming past or perhaps a whale staring back at you.

So again, I ask you: What must the Israelites have been thinking as they saw those waters rise? What kind of faith must it have taken to step on that path with a wall of water on each side? Hold on to that image! We must never, *never* lose the utter wonder and majesty of the miraculous in our lives. Throughout this book I mostly discuss the small, sometimes unnoticeable miracles that occur in the course of our daily lives. But again and again I will challenge you to put those "small" miracles in their greater context. God works in huge, supernatural, undeniable ways. The power that parted the Red Sea is the same power that works in the world today. It's the same power that works miracles in us and through us, no matter how significant (or insignificant) they appear at the time. The truth is, God still parts the waters for each of us every day, but *how* He does it changes all the time.

Sometimes God Shouts

God's parting the Red Sea for Moses and the Israelites is an example of what I call God "shouting." These are the miracles that are so big, so loud, so unmistakably obvious that you have no choice but to label them "miracles." We have said that a miracle can be defined as God stepping into the universal laws He created and altering the natural order of things for the benefit of His children. There can be no doubt that the parting of the Red Sea is an example of just this type of miracle.

Time after time throughout the Israelites' exodus, we see God throwing subtlety to the wind and moving in big, obvious ways (frogs and flies and locusts, oh my!). Why? Perhaps the frightened Israelites needed that kind of sign from heaven. They had suffered poverty and slavery for hundreds of years. They had all but forgotten God. And now, as the Lord was calling them out of slavery and into the new land He had prepared for them, perhaps He wanted to make it clear to them that the God they had forgotten was not only still with them, but was also willing to change the course of nature for their benefit. Their defeated spirits needed a big sign, so God shouted.

Sometimes God Speaks

Of course, God doesn't always shout. Sometimes, He simply speaks casually in the common encounters we have with people every day. For example, I love reading about Jesus' healing miracles in the Bible. What a perfect way to illustrate the intersection of divine power and human weakness. In the book of Luke, we see Jesus walking toward Jericho on His way to Jerusalem. As He neared the city, He encountered a beggar sitting just off the road. When the beggar called His name, Jesus stopped. The man had His attention. Don't miss the significance of this. Jesus was on His way to Jerusalem. His days were numbered. He was literally marching toward His death on the cross, but here, a poor, sick stranger called out to Him, and the Bible says that "Jesus stopped" and asked, "What do you want me to do for you?" (Luke 18:40–41). That kind of personal attention alone is miraculous to me!

The man made his simple request: He wanted to see. And, without hesitation, in full view and hearing of the crowd around him, Jesus said, "Receive your sight; your faith has healed you" (Luke 18:42). Immediately, light entered this man's eyes for the first time. Shapes came into focus. He could see the faces of the people who had been yelling at him to keep quiet moments earlier. He could see the complete shock on their faces as they realized they were witnesses to a mighty, dramatic, miraculous healing.

Sometimes God Whispers

My wife, Crystal, and I have a friend who experienced a type of "whisper miracle" in a dramatic way. Lynne Twist is a fabulous speaker and the author of the book *The Soul of Money*. She personally raised over $200 million for The Hunger Project, a global nonprofit organization committed to ending world hunger. As head of the project's fundraising efforts, Lynne was invited to Sierra Leone in Africa by the tribal chieftains because of an extensive and debilitating drought. When Lynne arrived, the chieftains requested $250,000 in order to build a well.

Lynne sensed an odd spirit about the place and about the men with whom she was dealing, so she asked to speak to the women of the tribe. The chieftains reacted with a strong chauvinistic attitude. They replied, "What could they possibly know? They are women!" She insisted, however, and was eventually given an audience with the women of the community.

As Lynne spoke personally with each of the women, she was shocked at the story they told. One lady told Lynne she had a dream about finding water in a specific spot in the village, fewer than twenty feet underground.

Lynne spoke to another woman and heard the exact same thing. Then another. Then another. Lynne and the women of the tribe realized that every single woman present had experienced the exact same dream, finding water in one specific spot.

Lynne returned to the chieftains and told them that she would indeed give them the money to dig a well, but only after they dug in the spot the women dreamed about. She was convinced in her spirit that something miraculous was happening. The men mocked Lynne and the other women. They refused to dig themselves, and demanded that the women dig instead. And, as an additional insult, the men only allowed the women to dig using spoons.

Undeterred, Lynne and the tribal women started digging with spoons in the spot they had all seen in their dreams. It took three days to dig to the twenty-foot mark, but can you guess what happened when they got there? Yes! These ladies hit the biggest oasis geyser in Africa!

God could have shouted by revealing the geyser through a mighty earthquake. He could have spoken by having it trickle to the surface seemingly out of nowhere one day. But this time He chose to whisper through the dreams of the most overlooked and ignored members of the community. He works in all three ways, and every one of them is miraculous.

Miraculous Possibilities

As we bring this first section of the book to a close, I pray that your eyes have opened to the possibility of miracles. The Bible is certainly filled with amazing tales of God acting in the world, but we must not allow ourselves to fall into the belief that miracles *only* happen in the pages of God's Word.

We must not allow ourselves to fall into the belief that miracles *only* happen in the pages of God's Word. Doing so robs the miracle passages of one of their greatest functions. You see, we must come to view these passages not as *stories*, but as *examples*.

Doing so robs the miracle passages of one of their greatest functions. You see, we must come to view these passages not as *stories*, but as *examples*. The Bible shows us how God has acted in the world of the past so that we can learn to see how He is acting in the world around us today.

In the foreword to this book, my friend Dr. Ben Carson wrote, "Whether or not one believes in miracles is immaterial. They occur whether you acknowledge them or not." How true! Your doubt in miracles does not slow them any more than your doubt in a river could slow its current. However, if you want to fully participate in the miracle-making process, you have to accept that God not only does miracles, but that He does them in *your life* just as He did in the lives of many in biblical times.

Third Miracle Scroll

I Am Miracle Minded

Miracles are fun to create because
I am miracle minded.
I have set my goals to create miracles.
Today and every day I can create exciting miracles.
I have plans to create more and more miracles.
From before my birth God planned on
creating miracles in me and through me.
I am reading this and being reminded
of the promise He made to me
even before I was born.

PART II

See the Miracle

4

Focusing on Miracles

My friend Mick Hall once told me about a terrifying near-death experience he had when he was thirteen years old. Having been raised on a family farm, young Mick was accustomed to hard work. Mick had been taught how to drive the family's 1932 Caterpillar Bulldozer D-6. That day, his job was to cut down some trees for the sawmill. So Mick jumped onto the seat of the Cat with his tools in hand, paying no attention to the expensive chainsaw that sat idle next to him on the seat. Mick turned on the giant Cat engine, which roared to life. Just as he put it in gear and released the master clutch—which took both hands and all his strength—the bulldozer violently lurched backward. What happened next must have only lasted mere seconds, but Mick recounts the story fifty years later with crystal clarity.

Miracles not only exist, but they happen both *to* you and *through* you. The form the miracle takes may be supernaturally obvious and awe-inspiring, or it may escape your attention entirely.

As the Cat lurched, the chainsaw was thrown up in the air. It immediately occurred to Mick that if the chainsaw fell behind the bulldozer, it would be crushed beneath the eight-ton machine's metal treads. Without thinking, Mick dove backward to catch the chainsaw, which caused him to lose his balance. Falling directly behind the bulldozer, right in the path of those dangerous treads, Mick says his life flashed before his eyes. His heart jumped into his throat, his pulse raced faster than he'd ever felt it, and sweat poured from his brow and body. He also heard the unmistakable sound of his inner being—his heart and mind—asking God to intercede.

Then, just as Mick hit the ground, just as he faced the mighty treads of an out-of-control bulldozer, everything stopped. His prayers had been answered! Mick believes that somehow, as a result of his desperate prayers, God delivered a life-saving miracle.

Reflecting on that day many years later, Mick said, "Here's what I thought: I didn't get crushed to death. I got badly bruised, but that would heal. I wouldn't make that mistake again. The chainsaw would still work for felling trees, I didn't wreck the Cat, and I didn't have to tell my folks how dumb I was. If I told them, they would have killed me—trying to avoid death twice in one day was more than I could handle! I kept quiet and told no one until now, fifty years later." As for the form the miracle took, Mick said, "My left boot must have hit the clutch and kicked it off as I was falling to my demise, thanks to my heartfelt prayer for immediate divine intervention.

Bringing Thought into Reality

Mick's story brings to mind an important point in the miracle discussion. Again and again in this book, I talk about what I call the miracle mindset. That is the intentional, willful belief that miracles not only exist, but they happen both *to* you and *through* you. The form the miracle takes may be supernaturally obvious and awe-inspiring, or it may escape your attention entirely and seem more like dumb luck. For those of us who are miracle-minded, dumb luck is not an option. We accept the fact that miracles come in all shapes and sizes. So, with that mindset firmly in place, let's see how to nourish and nurture the miracle mindset in your mind and spirit. There are, I believe, two keys to making this a reality: prayer and focus.

In the Bible, the book of Mark shows us a wonderful affirmation of this principle in the words and actions of Jesus. As Jesus and His disciples journeyed toward Jerusalem, He approached a fig tree to see if it had any fruit. Upon seeing it barren, He said to the tree, "May no one ever eat fruit from you again" (Mark 11:14). The passage also makes it clear that He said this loudly enough for the disciples to hear Him.

The next morning, as Jesus and the disciples were leaving Jerusalem, they passed back by the fig tree Jesus had cursed. The passage continues, "As they went along, they saw the fig tree withered from the roots. Peter remembered and said to Jesus, 'Rabbi, look! The fig tree you cursed has withered!'" (Mark 11:20–21). I often wonder, *Why was Peter so shocked?* After all, he had walked with Jesus, the true Miracle Maker.

Peter had seen Jesus perform amazing miracles, but he still seemed completely surprised by the withered fig tree.

Jesus' reply to His dumbfounded friend is especially meaningful to us as we seek to expand our miracle mindset:

"Have faith in God," Jesus answered. "Truly I tell you, if anyone says to this mountain, 'Go, throw yourself into the sea,' and does not doubt in their heart but believes that what they say will happen, it will be done for them. Therefore I tell you, whatever you ask for in prayer, believe that you have received it, and it will be yours" (Mark 11:22–24).

This is a powerful testimony to the intimate connection between our faith and our prayers. Of course, Jesus is not saying that we can speak any crazy whim into existence. The point is not to turn God into some sort of magic genie who is always on call to grant every wish and obey our every command. I believe Jesus is simply reframing the prayer/faith/miracle discussion for His companions. Somehow, they had grown more comfortable with the idea of a Savior who could heal the sick, give sight to the blind, and walk on water than they were a Savior who could bring the miraculous into the mundane—something as simple as causing a fig tree to die. In this scene, He reminded them that, in prayer, we all have access to the ultimate power of the universe, and that power is a Person who seeks to invade every part of our lives, big and small. Those invasions are called miracles.

When we focus our thoughts and prayers on something, we should not be surprised, as the disciples were, to find that miracles happen. Regarding this kind of experience, Bob Proctor says, "Prayer is the movement that takes place between spirit and form with and through you." Likewise, Andrew Carnegie once said, "Any idea that is held in the mind, that is emphasized, that is either feared or revered, will begin at once to clothe itself in the most convenient and appropriate form available." That is, what we focus our thoughts and prayers on has a miraculous way of becoming reality. We must not only *recognize* this truth, but *embrace* it, as well.

The Power of Focus

That Andrew Carnegie quote has been planted deep in my spirit. "Any idea held in the mind . . . will begin at once to clothe itself in the most convenient and appropriate form available." I remember when Jack Canfield and I were preparing to release the first *Chicken Soup for the Soul* book. So many publishers had turned us down, but we just kept trying. I maintained a laser focus on my goal, which was to make the book a number-one bestseller. To help make my goal more precise, I focused on one of our interview subjects, Dr. Scott Peck, author of *The Road Less Traveled*, a *New York Times* bestseller for twelve full years.

What we focus our thoughts and prayers on has a miraculous way of becoming reality. We must not only recognize this truth, but embrace it, as well.

I took a copy of that week's Sunday *New York Times* and whited out *The Road Less Traveled* on the bestsellers list. Then I wrote "*Chicken Soup for the Soul* by Mark Victor Hansen and Jack Canfield" in its place. I did that with four copies of the paper, and then I cut out the bestsellers lists with my modification. I put one of the "revised" lists on my office mirror for all the staff and visitors to see. I put another one on Jack's front office mirror, one at my home for my spouse and kids to see, and the last one at Jack's home.

The result? It worked. Our book became the all-time

bestselling book. We took ownership of that goal by focusing our thoughts on it. We kept that goal front and center for more than a year, and success followed. I was reminded of what my speech teacher, Cavett Robert, told me years earlier: "Once you know what you want, you will have it so quickly that it will amaze you." You don't have to know *how* this works; you just need to know that it *does* work.

Praying for Miracles

While I was focused on making our book a bestseller, I didn't just *think* about it; I *prayed* about it all the time! I talked to God about what we were doing, what we wanted to happen, what worried me about it, and what excited me about it. I prayed about the obstacles and the opportunities. I told God unashamedly that I wanted that book to be a number-one hit! Some people are uncomfortable with that. They act as though God doesn't want to hear about our passions and goals. Nothing could be further from the truth! Matthew 7:11 affirms that our heavenly Father loves giving good gifts to His children. Psalm 37:4 says, "Take delight in the LORD, and he will give you the desires of your heart." God hears our prayers, and those prayers in faith can unlock unbelievable miracles.

Tiffanie Rudgley and Cheree Swan certainly believe this to be true. Having watched her young daughter go through intense health problems as an infant, Cheree felt a deep call on her life to help other families in medical distress. After years of thought and prayer, Cheree decided to become a kidney donor. She did not have any particular donor in mind, so she went through the required testing and was added to the national donor list. At that point, there was nothing to do but wait for God to deliver the person He had selected to receive her life-saving gift. After a year of prayer, Cheree finally got the call that a recipient had been found, and things were set in motion. However, due to circumstances outside her control, the transplant fell through. Cheree was crushed to learn that she had to keep waiting for a new recipient for the gift she wanted so badly to give.

Soon after, Cheree attended a new ladies Bible study and prayer group at a local church at the invitation of a friend. She mentioned to the group that she was a registered kidney donor and that her plans for donation had recently fallen through. She and the group prayed together, asking God to bring His chosen recipient to her soon.

The lady sitting next to her, Tiffanie Rudgley, had been burdened with an urgent prayer request of her own for weeks.

Tiffanie's husband, Shance, was dealing with end-stage renal disease. He had been on dialysis for more than a year and desperately needed a kidney transplant. Tiffanie's family had been praying throughout their ordeal for a match to pop up on the donor list, but months went by without a call. Time was running out.

So here were two ladies who had never met. Both were first-time attenders to this Bible study. Both had been praying daily for God to answer their prayers, to give them the deep desires of their hearts. Both had a desperate need—one to give a kidney, and the other to find a kidney. Can you guess what happened next?

Yes! The ladies began talking and soon Cheree was tested to see if she was a match for Tiffanie's husband. The result: perfect match! Out of more than ninety-eight thousand people on the kidney donor list, the perfect donor had simply walked in off the street and taken a seat next to Tiffanie in a ladies' Bible study. Despite the overwhelming evidence, I suppose there are some that would call that a coincidence, but you and I know better. This was a miracle in its purest form, the direct result of God answering the fervent prayers of His children.

Tuning Your Mind Toward Miracles

The power of prayer and focus absolutely cannot be under-estimated. Where you focus your thoughts directs the whole course of your life and, therefore, your future. And this is key: You can control what you focus on. Of course, you can't control what pops into your mind, but you certainly can control what you do with it once it's there. As Martin Luther famously said, "You can't stop birds from flying over your head, but you can keep them from making a nest in your hair!"

Have you ever noticed that if you wake up angry for some reason, everything that happens that day enrages you? But, if you wake up feeling positive and lock on to that feeling, things seem to go your way that day. What's changed? You could have the exact same experiences with totally different outcomes. It's your state of mind, not your circumstances, that dictates whether it will be a good day or a bad day. So here is my challenge for you: Take control of your thoughts and prayers and focus them toward positive outcomes for thirty-one days. If you willfully sustain that positive, hopeful outlook for thirty-one days in a row, you can be pretty much locked and loaded for life as a positive, optimistic, upbeat person who gets results. Yes, it takes discipline to reach the thirty-one-day mark, and it won't always be easy to reset your mind. But, my friend, the exercise is totally worth it! Your life will look miraculous!

Fourth Miracle Scroll

I Am a Unique Miracle

I am a unique miracle, unlike any other—ever.

My soul is a miracle.

My mind is a thinking miracle.

My brain is an inventory miracle.

My emotions are a guidance miracle.

My eyes are a miracle. My ears are a miracle.

My hands are a miracle. My mouth is a miracle.

My skin is a miracle. My body is a miracle.

My walking is a miracle. My talking is a miracle.

My thinking is a miracle. My ability to be is a miracle.

My ability to do is a miracle.

My ability to have is a miracle.

My ability to serve greatly is a miracle.

My ability to love is a miracle.

5

Looking for Miracles

I f you were to ask me what the greatest miracle of my life was, I could easily sum it up in one word: Crystal. You see, I am *more* than a happily married man; I am a *joyfully* married man. I realize that not everyone can say that. My wife, Crystal, and I have what I call a "twin flame relationship." Twin flames positively and correctly mirror each other in near-perfect harmony. They experience and express a delightful, divine destiny together. They desire to be, do, and have as much for their partner as for themselves. They think and act alike in many ways, yet are strong where the other is weak. The twin flame relationship is one in which their individual qualities compliment and complete their circle of love. And just as when two candle flames merge, twin flames understand that by coming together, their joined flame burns brighter and with more intensity than they ever could alone. What we share is truly a miracle that is renewed every morning.

A Very Specific Miracle Prayer

There was a time when I didn't think such a miraculous marriage was possible. I went through a season of grief and mild depression after the painful end of my first marriage. Even with scores of friends around me, it felt frighteningly lonely not to be in a marriage anymore. I realized that being married to a true soul mate had been a top priority my entire life, but my failed marriage had cast a long shadow over my heart. Through much prayer, I kept coming back to the thought that God had painted on my heart long ago, that my soul mate was still out there somewhere, and that I would find her. I started to dream of the perfect woman and to focus intently on exactly the qualities and outcomes I most desired. I sat down and wrote out a detailed list of 267 qualities and characteristics that I desired in my future soul mate. I prayed over that list endlessly, always asking God to show me if I need to add or remove something from my "dream list." I shared the list with my closest friends and prayer partners but no one else. Finding the lady I was describing seemed to border on the impossible, but I clung to the promise God had imprinted upon me. I knew she was out there and, in His timing, I would find her.

A short time later, I was speaking at an aspiring writer's conference in Los Angeles. From the stage, I clearly saw a radiant spirit of a woman in the middle of the audience. I was so drawn to what I saw. She made a dynamic, lasting, and irresistible first impression. After my talk, as I was greeting what seemed like an endless stream of eager writers in the VIP reception, this beautiful lady once again caught my attention. I had learned her name was Crystal and that she was at the conference alone. I wanted so badly to speak to her, but there was no way to politely cut off the people who had lined up to speak to me. I quietly prayed for a miracle— and God responded! Across the room, much to my delight, I saw another attendee wave her arms and inadvertently knock over a full glass of red wine, dousing Crystal's white slacks. It was a beautiful, miraculous mess!

I dashed to Crystal's side and offered my assistance. Since I had spoken at that particular hotel several times, I knew how to get through the ballroom and into the kitchen. I walked her back there to get some club soda for her to use in cleaning her terribly stained slacks. As we chatted, I asked her if she wanted to continue the conversation over dinner. She agreed, and we began an amazing courtship.

Through much prayer, I kept coming back to the thought that God had painted on my heart long ago, that my soul mate was still out there somewhere, and that I would find her.

At first I thought this miracle was unfolding only in my life, but I soon discovered our relationship was an answer to prayer in Crystal's life as well, as she also was struggling through a failed marriage and a broken heart. In her own words, this is the miracle she was experiencing:

After a particularly long day of sorting through details of the finalizing of my divorce, what to do with property, and concerns about the kids, college trips, and the like, I fell into bed exhausted and went into deep sleep. In the wee hours of the morning I awoke from a dream that was so profound and so unlike any I'd ever had that I knew God was trying to communicate with me.

In my dream, I was walking side by side with Mark in a beautiful mountain retreat. The feeling was that we'd just facilitated a life-changing conference together, concluding the day with a time of answering questions and reacting to comments from the attendees. As we all walked back to our cabins, which lined both sides of a narrow road under the beautiful starry sky, Mark and I felt a sense of extreme urgency and desire to be together alone. It was a holistic feeling that we needed to merge at the deepest level of body, mind, and spirit. We were both relieved when the last person fell away and we were alone at last under the stars.

As I looked up into the sky, I saw a beautiful pink star, which started zooming toward us. I said, "Mark, look!" As the star got closer and closer, it became bigger and bigger until it was right in front of us, touching the ground, bigger than both of us. Mark shirked back, startled, so I reached over and grabbed his hand

and said, "Don't be afraid. Just look into the center. It's gathering information about us, determining that we can influence so many people's lives for the better." And then I woke up.

The dream and all of the feelings and understandings inside of it profoundly moved me. I kept asking God what it meant about me and this man I'd only had one meal with. The answer was there almost before I asked. It seemed impossible that I could have met the person I was supposed to spend the rest of my life with. I wasn't even planning to officially begin dating yet! Even though I knew I needed to keep the order I had planned with my kids, I had a deep confirmation and knowing as I prayed to God throughout that day, that my life had changed permanently from that meeting, and that something profoundly amazing and special was coming.

When Mark and I did begin officially dating that fall, even though we both had our old baggage to let go of, again and again God kept confirming to each of us that we had found our soul mate in each other. We committed our lives to each other and got married two and a half years later, after my kids graduated from high school and launched into college. We both agree and affirm every day, that everything about my being at that event, our meeting, the dream that showed us a piece of our amazing future, and all of the other little things along the way, were nothing short of God's divine love intervening on our behalf, to help us find our true love in life. It was nothing less than a magnificent miracle. The beautiful thing is, we get to live the miracle each and every day!

During the course of our courtship, I discovered that this amazing woman was handpicked by God to be my soul mate. She not only embodied every quality that my friends and I had prayed for; she was so much more than I ever could have dreamed! Finally, under the majestic red rocks of Sedona, Arizona, we were joyfully married.

I tell you this story because I believe it demonstrates an important point in our miracle discussion. And that is, miracles happen to us every day; however, we often turn a blind eye to the incredible daily miracles that add up to a wonderfully fulfilling and beautiful life! The vision God put in my heart of my soul mate was a miracle. His comfort, strength, and support during my divorce and recovery was a miracle.

The list of qualities He gave me to pray about was a miracle. The burning hope for true love despite my deep heartache and loneliness was a miracle. Bringing me to speak at that writer's conference in L.A.; shining an unmistakable light on Crystal across a crowded room; even knocking a glass of wine out of someone's hand and onto her slacks . . . Miracles!

Miracles happen to us every day; however, we often turn a blind eye to the incredible daily miracles that add up to a wonderfully fulfilling and beautiful life! The vision God put in my heart of my soul mate was a miracle.

But what would have happened if I had ignored each piece of the puzzle He was putting together? What if I had not viewed these things through the miracle mindset, but instead dismissed them as trivial, coincidental, or random occurrences? I shudder even to consider it. Looking back over the course of my life, I see an endless string of unmistakable miracles leading me right into Crystal's arms. And, praise God, I was able to move from one miracle to the next as God wove this love story together!

One Miracle Inspires Another

Matthew Ferry's life was unbelievably busy between marriage, raising four kids, building a new business—and all the financial worries that come with it. He had no time to do the one thing he loved doing—create music. It had been years since he had made his last album, and although the thought of doing another one was constantly on his mind, fitting it into his schedule seemed nearly impossible. He recalls:

Some songs were coming, but I was ready for the next one. *I need a miracle*, I thought to myself. I don't need the seas to part. I need the powerful energy of inspiration. I soon realized the reason I wasn't experiencing a breakthrough or a miracle in this area of my life was because my focus was on myself and my business. I was trying to fill a hole in my soul with success, material possessions, and doing the right thing in other people's eyes. But whatever the gain I was experiencing in that area of my life only exposed how much was missing from my life in other areas. My inner voice was yelling, *Contribute! Make a difference! Take your focus off of your needs and see how you can help other people!* Wow! That's what was missing when it came to expressing myself musically! It's time to take my focus off of myself and see how I can help others.

Miraculously, that was about the time Crystal and I had been dating and preparing to get married. Not realizing it, I guess I told Matthew multiple times the story of how I kept asking Crystal to marry me over and over again because I loved hearing her say yes. Matthew continued:

Mark was dazzled by the miracle that she said yes. And that was my miracle. *Kabam!* The inspiration hit. What if I take their beautiful and romantic story and create a song for them as a wedding gift? Nothing in it for me. Just the joy of creating something that will memorialize their beautiful story. A torrent of energy surged through me. With the unstoppable energy of a tsunami, the words and melody started flooding into my mind. I quickly connected with my writing partner David Keesee, and my inspiration sparked his creativity. Within forty-eight hours the entire song was done. The seas of life did part. The noise and distraction disappeared. God's force, inspiration, and creativity flowed through, and a wonderful song came into being.

You never know when a miracle is going to happen. And you never know when the miracle you have been looking for reveals another miracle being sought by another. By the way, go to **markandcrystalsong.com** and enjoy having, listening, and sharing Matthew's song for free.

Keeping Your Eyes Open

I truly believe one of the keys to success in our marriages, careers, relationships, and every other area is disciplining ourselves to look for the miracles in life. I refuse to believe that anything happens to us by chance; therefore, each event or encounter, no matter how seemingly random, must have some meaning. That means we have to be vigilant to watch for the miracles that God brings our way each and every day.

Of course, keeping your eyes open to God's often-subtle interventions takes time. This is a new skill you're learning, and you won't be an expert overnight. In fact, Crystal and I take this so seriously that we dedicate the first hour of our day together in prayer and meditation. Much of that time is spent focusing on our marriage and our shared goals for the rest of our lives. But we also spend that time quietly reflecting on what's going on in our lives, who God has brought into view, what new opportunities seem to be coming to the surface, and so on.

Day after day, God opens our eyes to all sorts of new miracles, simply because we have disciplined ourselves to *look*. Most people spend so much time praying for the miracles they *think they want* that they have no clear vision of the miracles God is *already doing* in their lives!

Finding Miracles in Unexpected Places

If learning to look for miracles is a challenge for the average person, learning how to see them from the inside of a prison cell must seem impossible. And yet, that's exactly where Bill Sands discovered the most life-changing miracle of his life. And that miracle came in an unlikely form: his captor.

Growing up, Bill's dad was a well-known judge who was strict on the bench and a tyrant at home. Feeling neglected and seeking attention from his father, Bill did what he thought would get the judge's attention: he broke the law—*repeatedly*. By age nineteen, Bill found himself in San Quentin Prison doing an extremely long and hard sentence. And yet, thirty years later, Bill had become a super successful businessman, famous speaker, best-selling author, pilot, boxer, comedian, and even a diamond miner! He lived an extraordinary life and, when he died, he left a legacy of stories, dreams, and belief that life can always get better.

How did it happen? One day the warden at San Quentin, a man named Clinton Duffy, said, "I care, Bill." That alone was a miracle to this young, hurting, lonely criminal who had sought his father's approval his entire life. But Duffy continued, "Bill, you're better than this. Read this book, *Think and Grow Rich* by Napoleon Hill. Let's get you out of the slammer and making a difference." Those words turned Bill Sands completely around. From that point on, he became the model prisoner, which led to his early release. The principles Bill learned allowed him to take control of his life and future. Bill worked hard, studied, built wealth, and wrote a bestseller. Seeking to be a miracle to other convicts, Bill developed a powerful mentoring program for use inside prisons, which sought to lead men and women out of these institutions and end the cycle of recidivism.

As a speaker, Bill Sands' powerful talks showed millions of listeners that there was hope no matter how low you felt. More than that, he showed each person that they could live up to their full potential. Bill dedicated himself to making the world better for this and future generations. Truly, Bill became a miracle maker in every sense of the word, but it happened only because he first recognized the miracle in his own life. The miracle of a loving and encouraging prison warden changed not just one life but, through Bill, the lives of millions of others—including me. I had the honor of spending time with Bill Sands when he spoke at my college when I was a student. The day I spent with Bill has stuck with me, and his lessons have definitely made an impact not only on me but on everyone I've spoken to since. The miracle he experienced lives on, and you can read more about it in his book *My Shadow Ran Fast*.

Seeing Miracles Takes Time

It's one thing to say we need to become more mindful in looking for miracles; it's quite another to actually have the patience to do so. We lead such busy lives. Life moves past us so quickly, doesn't it? Isn't that what new parents hear from their older friends upon the birth of a child: "Pay attention, because it all goes by so fast." Plus, we are living in a world marked by instant gratification. Children born today will never know what it was like to live in a time when the answer to any question was not simply a click away. What chance do we have to see the miracles in our lives if we can't slow down long enough to pay attention?

It's one thing to say we need to become more mindful in looking for miracles; it's quite another to actually have the patience to do so.

The case for slow, mindful meditation is made perfectly by Rabbi Lawrence Kushner in his appropriately titled book *God Was in This Place and I, I Did Not Know.* In contemplating the story of Moses and the burning bush, Rabbi Kushner writes about how we often see the miracle in this story as the burning bush itself—how God so creatively got Moses' attention.

Kushner wonders, though, why God—who has done so many incredibly amazing miracles, such as parting the Red Sea so the Israelites could pass through or making the sun stand still—would not go to greater lengths to really wow Moses. Sure, a burning bush (which doesn't burn up) is cool, but God could have gone much, much bigger, don't you think? God is up to so much more than meets the eye. Here's what Kushner says:

How long would you have to watch wood burn before you could know whether or not it actually was being consumed? Even dry kindling wood is not burned up for several minutes. This then would mean that Moses would have had to watch the "amazing sight" closely for several minutes before he could possibly know that there was even a miracle to watch! [The producers of television commercials, who have a lot invested in knowing the span of human visual attention, seem to agree that one minute is our outer limit.]

The burning bush was not a miracle. It was a test. God wanted to find out whether or not Moses could pay attention to something for more than a few minutes. When Moses did, God spoke. The trick is to pay attention to what is going on around you long enough to behold the miracle without falling asleep. There is another world, right here within this one, whenever we pay attention.[2]

Those are haunting words, are they not? Read the last lines again, slowly this time: "The trick is to pay attention to what is going on around you long enough to behold the miracle without falling asleep. There is another world, right here within this one, whenever we pay attention."

And that, my friend, is the hardest part about looking for miracles. They are all around. God is always speaking, moving, and acting on our behalf. He wants so desperately for us to join Him in that activity, but first, we have to learn to *see* where He is moving and what He is doing. To that end, I beg you to slow down! Sit still! Dedicate part of your day, even if it is only a few minutes, to prayer and meditation, asking God to open your eyes to His wondrous work in your life. As Psalm 46:10 instructs, "Be still, and know that I am God." That is not only our challenge; it is our *imperative* if we are to become true miracle makers in this world.

Fifth Miracle Scroll

I Expect Miracles

I feel, believe, and expect miracles.

God's promises are the same

yesterday, today, and tomorrow.

God's miracles were fully displayed through

Moses, David, Solomon, and Jesus,

and what God has done for them

He will do through me.

My future is miraculous.

I have a miraculous certainty

in business and in life.

I am certain that my problems are

opportunities in disguise.

I am here to become one of God's greatest miracles.

I was created in God's image, and He is in me.

I feel the breath of God in me now and always.

6

Doubting Miracles

J uly 2, 1993. That's the day I died."

Don Gandy was hopeless. Over the past year, the college senior's joy and zest for life had been eaten away bit by bit. He had been removed from his position as president of his fraternity due to an unfortunate campus-wide scandal. He suffered the agonizing loss of a childhood friend. He was under a seemingly insurmountable pile of debt in the form of student loans—to the tune of thirty thousand dollars. He recalls, "I felt completely hopeless, like I had no way to manage, let alone pay off, all of this debt. I saw no way out."

Hiding behind his trademark smile and good humor (his college nickname was "Happy"), Don finally hit rock bottom in June 1993. "I truly felt that I could not go on and had no end in sight. Finally, I decided that I was done. I tried to think of a way to end it all. I even went out and bought a book on the different ways to commit suicide. I read that book from cover to cover and was trying to come up with the perfect way to end it all." The pressure built up for a few weeks, until finally the day arrived. "July 2, 1993. That's the day I died. I remember [waking up and] thinking, *Today is the day.*"

Despite his study of suicide methods, Don didn't know exactly how he wanted to end his life. He was consumed with the idea of his hopeless escape as he drove around town. Then, while sitting at a stoplight near his home, Don looked up and saw the local bank. That's when the decision was made: Don was going to rob the bank. "I took my BB gun pistol out of my trunk and tucked it into my pants under my shirt. I walked into the bank with the intention of being shot to death by the police at some point during the robbery. I thought that I could at least go out in a blaze of glory, like in a good western," he explains.

The plan, however, did not turn out as he expected. Rather than sounding the alarm, the teller simply handed him the money. As he drove away bewildered, the dye pack exploded in his car. The police soon caught up to the still-smoking getaway vehicle, and Don was sent to jail. He was ultimately sentenced to forty-one months in a federal facility, and he was required to serve at least thirty-six months of his sentence. For a young man with a death wish, three years seemed like an eternity. Don's hopelessness only grew darker.

Don Gandy's prison term began on May 14, 1994. He entered the system in a state of depression, fright, and despair. He had been abandoned by most of his friends, and any hope for a "normal" life after prison seemed remote at best. He focused on building up his mental and emotional defenses for life in prison. But then, something unexpected happened. He explains, "I got a letter one day from a man I had never met about a month into my sentence. He said that he had met my mom at church and that he wanted to write to me while I was in prison. I was really on guard with this prison mindset at the time and thought, *Yeah, what does this guy want from me? No thanks.* So, I just ignored it."

A few days later, another letter arrived from this man— and was ignored. A few days later, he received yet another letter. "These were really long letters, and I was getting two or three a week. He would just talk and talk to me like we had known each other for years. I started to trust him, so I wrote back." The man on the other end of this life-giving conversation was named Paul and, despite Don's deep doubt and strong defenses, he had become Don's miracle. Weeks turned into months, and this unending conversation brought ever-increasing light into Don's darkness. The men discussed faith, God's plan for Don's life, and Jesus' sacrifice for Don's sins. Three months into Don's prison term, he embraced the biggest miracle of life: salvation through Christ.

Despite Don's deep doubt and strong defenses, he had become Don's miracle. Weeks turned into months, and this unending conversation brought ever-increasing light into Don's darkness.

After that miraculous encounter, and through Paul's miraculous friendship, Don's three years in prison were spent in prayer and Bible study, as Don looked to the future with something he never expected to find inside a prison cell: hope.

Finally, the day of his release arrived. "Some friends and

family met me at the prison to drive me to the halfway house. On the way, we stopped at Paul's house. We had been close friends for over two years, and I thought it was time that we actually met. I just hugged him and thanked him for his friendship and faithfulness. He literally saved my life."

Don's life in the years since has been marked by miracle after miracle. He is happily married, has had a successful career, and is the proud father of a wonderful little boy. Thinking back over his amazing, unexpected life, Don Gandy reflects, "God gives us the right to make our own decisions. That's a gift, but it means we can really mess up our lives with bad choices. *The miracle happens, however, when God steps in and somehow guides us down the path He had planned for us all along, despite our biggest mistakes."*

Finding Hope in Hopelessness

Don's story is just one of the thousands I've heard that demonstrates the amazing power of God to infiltrate a seemingly hopeless life. Too often we allow the darkness around us to blind us to God's miraculous interventions. We allow depression, disappointment, anxiety, fear, regret, and a million other emotions to crowd out the voice that whispers, "This is the way; walk in it" (Isaiah 30:21). Of course, I would never minimize the deep sorrow that accompanies depression, and I would never suggest an "easy" answer to that kind of hopelessness. However, I also cannot ignore God's willingness to reach into our darkness supernaturally or with the miracle-making hands of another person.

In the midst of our despair, He is still bringing miracles into our lives. That is His promise to us. That is why it is so important to cling to the miracle mindset, even in the midst of doubt.

Jeremiah 29:11 boldly proclaims, "'For I know the plans I have for you,' declares the LORD, 'plans to prosper you and not to harm you, plans to give you hope and a future.'" That phrasing is so important. God doesn't say He will allow us to *find* hope or that He will allow us to *stumble into* hope. No, the God of the universe declares that He will *give* us hope! Whether we are looking for it or not, whether we believe in it or not, our heavenly Father is actively working on our behalf. He has not abandoned us! In the midst of our despair, He is still bringing miracles into our lives. That is His promise to us. That is why it is so important to cling to the miracle mindset, even in the midst of doubt. The miracles are still happening; we just may not be able to see them for a season.

Responding to Doubt

Years ago, my friend Dr. Asher Milgrom was lost in a maze of fear and uncertainty. He was on the cusp of something unbelievable. God's rich blessings were poised to rain down like Asher had never known. And yet, my friend was almost paralyzed with doubt.

Dr. Milgrom had spent the last two years chasing down what he thought was a magnificent opportunity in the jungles of Belize. He and a group of colleagues had devised a plan to create an offshore medical practice specializing in cosmetic surgery that would cater to the world's elite. Their idea was to create a type of destination resort to which high-end patients would fly to have their procedures done in a private paradise. It seemed like such low-hanging fruit that Asher was convinced this was an opportunity sent straight from heaven. And yet, after a solid year of fruitless meetings, the dream faded into oblivion buried under a morass of legal complications and contentious business wrangling. By the second year, all hope for the project seemed lost.

But then, the real stream of miracles began. First, the

owner of the most exquisite resort in the region offered to sell a perfect tract of riverfront property for a fantastic price. The land was perfect for a medical center! Then, like falling dominos, previously impenetrable obstacles such as legal, banking, accounting, and regulatory issues were effortlessly dissolved by suddenly helpful and encouraging government officials. It seemed for a season that the cosmetic surgery center was becoming a reality! But, as it happened, that's not at all what was taking shape.

As the different pieces fell into place, another reality was forming in Asher's heart. Suddenly, he became painfully aware of the dismal state of healthcare in Central America. The vast majority of these warm and charismatic people had virtually no basic healthcare. In fact, modern medicine was barely present in the region. The progression of falling dominos stopped, as Dr. Milgrom realized his entire dream was about to change. The plans for a cosmetic surgery center were radically altered, as Asher focused instead on creating a full medical missionary program with a goal of not only serving the community's basic medical needs, but also providing training and education for the nation's doctors and nurses. What started as a narrow offering of only cosmetic surgery for the world's elite had instead become a resource for education, specialty treatment, and basic healthcare.

The miracles resumed. When faced with the challenge of how to fund such a massive endeavor, Asher was stunned when the answer practically fell in his lap. Completely unsolicited, a large contingent of foreign residents—mostly wealthy, retired U.S. and Canadian citizens—brought a lucrative proposal. If the medical group would provide a concierge medical program to their specialized community, the foreign nationals would pay a hefty fee that would support the entire medical center into perpetuity! God's miraculous provision was evident to all . . . except Dr. Milgrom.

He recalls, "I was now on my own. Everything was falling into place, only this time around, the project depended on me—and that is where the obstacles and resistance that were magically absent elsewhere began to menacingly show up. That very night, my dreams were filled with images of an inquisition under whose searing scrutiny I was being challenged. *Do you actually think you are the one to make this happen? Could this plan of yours really be that good? Are expert physicians really going to join you in this mission? Are you really good enough to offer so much value to so many?*"

He continues, "The torrent of incisions was endless, and with the familiarity of an internal voice, each found its mark with excruciating precision. *You have made so many mistakes. You have had major failures. You have so many flaws.* Humiliated, broken, and alone, I was unable to stand for myself."

As Asher related his dream to me at the time, I was able to speak words of affirmation into his doubts. God put two simple words on my heart to share with my friend: "Of course."

Of course you have made many mistakes, *of course* you have doubts, *of course* you have many flaws, but also . . . *Of course* all your experiences in life have been a part of God's design to make you the man you are today, worthy of the miracle of this medical project! *Of course* you are the one to make this happen. *Of course* your plan is really that good. *Of course* other doctors will join you on this mission. *Of course* you are good enough.

With that, with those two simple words uttered in love and friendship, Asher was able to face the rising tide of doubt and embrace the fact that God wasn't just doing miracles *around* him; God was doing miracles *for* him. When Dr. Milgrom was reminded that God's hand was at work in and through him, the last domino fell into place. Three months later, the project received unanimous approval from all ministries of the Belizean government, and Dr. Asher Milgrom's medical center was recognized as establishing the foundation for the future of medicine throughout Central America. *Of course* it was!

Men like Don Gandy and Asher Milgrom remind me, in my own times of doubt and fear, that God is still at work. He has a plan, and His plan *will* be done. The miracles don't stop simply because we are occasionally unable to see or grasp them. And ultimately, it is our ability to not only *see* but also to *receive* the miracles in our own lives that—no matter the obstacles—position us to truly *become* the miracle for others.

Sixth Miracle Scroll

I Start Each Day with Love

I will greet this day creating miracles

out of the love in my heart.

My heart is full of love and overflowing

with miracle-making power.

I will use *Love*—

the greatest force in the *Universe*—

to conquer all,

for no hatred can defend itself against *Love*.

PART III

Be the Miracle

7

Called to Make Miracles

When we read the stories of the great miracle-making men and women in the Bible, our minds play a little trick on us. If we go back and read the first appearance of young David, the shepherd, in 1 Samuel 16, we already know he would one day slay the giant. If we turn to the very end of Genesis 5 and see the introduction of a man named Noah, we already know that God would work through him to restore and repopulate the entire earth. If we read about Moses' birth in Exodus 2, we already know that God would use him to free the entire nation of Israel in dramatic fashion. Therein lies our problem: *We already know.*

Here is a little secret about the great heroes of the Bible: They didn't know what miracles God was calling them to. When young David was in the field with his sheep or when James and John were tending their fishing nets, they had no idea what God had in store for them.

Joseph was a dreamer. Esther was an orphan. The apostle Paul was a persecutor. Peter, James, and John were fishermen. Matthew was a tax collector. But that's not how we remember them, is it? We remember them for what happened later, for what God empowered them to accomplish throughout their lives. We know the *end* of their stories, and that changes how we view the *beginning* of their stories.

But here is a little secret about the great heroes of the Bible: They didn't know what miracles God was calling them to. When young David was in the field with his sheep or when James and John were tending their fishing nets, they had no idea what God had in store for them. They didn't know that God was already at work preparing them to accomplish world-shaping miracles that impact us still today, these many thousands of years later. They just didn't know.

Created for Miracles

Please allow me to give you now what those famous miracle workers didn't have then: perspective. You, my friend, were born for miracles. You were born for greatness. The seeds of success were planted within you before the creation of the world! The apostle Paul writes:

> But because of his great love for us, God, who is rich in mercy, made us alive with Christ even when we were dead in transgressions—it is by grace you have been saved. And God raised us up with Christ and seated us with him in the heavenly realms in Christ Jesus, in order that in the coming ages he might show the incomparable riches of his grace, expressed in his kindness to us in Christ Jesus. For it is by grace you have been saved, through faith—and this is not from yourselves, it is the gift of God—not by works, so that no one can boast. For we are God's handiwork, created in Christ Jesus to do good works, which God prepared in advance for us to do (Ephesians 2:4–10).

Did you hear that? We are not only God's handiwork, but we are created to do good works. Miracles are in our nature! It's one of the reasons we were put on this planet! And these aren't just random miracles; they were prepared for us before the beginning of the world!

Let that sink in for just a minute. At the moment of Creation, God not only knew us, but He also knew the work He was calling us to do. That means every act of blessing we give to someone is a testimony to and an expression of the power of God. He knows *us*. He knows *our brothers and sisters*. He knows *their needs*, and He knows how to use *us* to meet them. That calling has been within us from the beginning, whether we have embraced it before or not! And this is not limited to a chosen few of us. This miracle-making potential lies at the heart of who we are as members of the human race, all seven billion of us walking around on this planet. Can you imagine what would happen if everyone on earth finally recognized and embraced their miracle-making calling? It would be incredible!

Blessed to Be a Blessing

We have a biblical mandate to bless other people. As God said to Abraham, "I will bless you; I will make your name great, and you will be a blessing" (Genesis 12:2). We have received God's blessings, and we are to pour out God's blessing upon others. We are *blessed to be a blessing.*

There is no feeling on earth like the satisfaction of making an impact on someone else. I've seen this time and again in a million ways great and small.

Now, does that mean our miracle making has to be a chore? Of course not! It is one of the greatest joys of my life! There is no feeling on earth like the satisfaction of making an impact on someone else. I've seen this time and again in a million ways great and small. You don't have to start by changing the world. You might just start by blessing an unsuspecting waitress with an unusually large tip the next time you go out to eat. That may not sound altogether miraculous to you, but it could be of immense value to her. Remember, God's prepared those works in advance for you to do. If you feel burdened to do something even only slightly out of the ordinary, listen to that impulse! That could very well be the God of the universe tapping on your shoulder to get your attention! Just like the heroes of the

Bible, you never know what the end result of your actions will be.

A Miraculous Thread

You have likely never heard of Edward Kimball. In the mid-nineteenth century, Edward was a simple Sunday school teacher at the Mt. Vernon Congregational Church in Boston. He loved the boys in his class, and he faithfully taught the Bible to them week after week. There was one teenager in particular who stood out to Edward. The child didn't really seem to want to be at church, which actually turned out to be true. The boy was only there because his uncle, with whom he lived, required it. So every week, Edward would teach from the Bible, and every week, this one teen seemed to drift further and further away.

Over time, Edward felt an undeniable urge to impact this young man's life. He was overcome with the sense that there was something he was supposed to do. So, even though he was painfully shy, he made the uncharacteristic decision to visit the teenager at his uncle's shoe store, where he worked. After nervously pacing back and forth outside the shop, Edward went in and asked the boy directly to become a Christian. By Edward's recollection, the conversation didn't go very well and he left feeling like he hadn't made a difference at all. He could not have been more wrong!

That young man, Dwight "D. L." Moody, had been listening. And as Edward Kimball shared with him, Dwight's flickering spirit exploded to life! It was a night and day difference. Before, he was described as "spiritually dark" and unable to understand anything about the faith. But now, not too long after his encounter with Kimball, Moody could not stop talking about Jesus. He felt compelled to tell everyone he knew about the decision he had made for Christ. A short time later, after moving to Chicago, it was said that Moody did not let a day go by without telling at least one person about Jesus. He had received a miracle through Edward Kimball's testimony, and he almost immediately began passing that miracle on to others!

D. L. Moody went on to be one of the most well-known evangelists in history. He founded the Moody Church, Moody Bible Institute, and Moody Publishers. As many as one million people are estimated to have come into a relationship with Jesus as a result of Moody's preaching, and his style and passion changed the shape of American evangelism forever.

Now, if this story ended there, it would still be remarkable and inspiring. After all, the impact of the miracles God works through us can be shockingly dramatic. Edward Kimball never imagined what the result of his nervous conversation in that shoe store would be. Leading one of the world's greatest evangelists to Christ changed the world! But let's not stop there. Remember, the miracles we see recorded in Scripture didn't just impact one person or even one generation; the effects rippled throughout all of history. So, let's follow some of the ripples in Edward Kimball's story.

Eighteen years after his conversion to Christianity, D. L. Moody left America to begin an evangelistic crusade in Liverpool, England. While there, he preached at a Baptist church pastored by F. B. Meyer. The two struck up a friendship, and Moody invited Meyer to come speak to some American crowds. Present at one of Meyer's American crusades was a young preacher named Wilber Chapman, who became so inspired by Meyer's preaching that he became an effective traveling evangelist himself. Later, Chapman was joined in his evangelistic crusade by a recent convert to Christianity named Billy Sunday. Over the years, Sunday himself became one of the leading evangelists in American history and led many thousands to Christ. During a preaching tour in North

Carolina, Sunday invited evangelist Mordecai Ham to conduct a crusade in Charlotte. Although the sessions frustrated Ham, he continued to pray for a miracle. His prayers were more than answered one night in 1934 when a sixteen-year-old local boy came up after the service to accept the preacher's call to Christ. The boy's name was William Franklin Graham, Jr.—but you probably know him as Billy.

Billy Graham, of course, is the best-known evangelist in history, and possibly the best-known Christian of modern times. It is estimated that more than three million people have received Jesus as a result of Graham's evangelistic crusades, and his lifetime radio and television audience is in excess of two billion people.[3] He has been a close friend and advisor to several American presidents. He has appeared on Gallup's list of most admired people a total of fifty-five times—more than anyone else in history. Few men have done more to change the religious, social, and political landscape of their time. As I write this, Billy Graham is in his late nineties and no doubt nearing the end of his remarkable life. However, his mission and ministry lives on not only through his children, who now run his Billy Graham Evangelistic Association, but also through the billions of people who have been touched by this one man. History will no doubt record many more miracles still to come as a result of Billy Graham's obedience to God's miracle-making call.

You don't know how one miracle will lead to the next, but history demonstrates that they flow one to another.
Your obedience today to become the miracle maker God has called you to be has the potential to literally change the world!

But let's not allow ourselves to be blinded by the work and notoriety of this one man. Yes, he has lived a historic life full of miracles and wonder, but it didn't start with Billy Graham. You can trace the thread of miracles at least one hundred and sixty years in the past, all the way back to one nervous Sunday school teacher who faithfully followed the call to minister to one seemingly lost shoe store clerk. And, of course, that's just where we began this story. We have no idea what miracle led up to Edward Kimball's life, or what miracle happened before then, or what miracle happened before then.

That's the thing about miracles. You don't know how one

miracle will lead to the next, but history demonstrates that they flow one to another. Your obedience today to become the miracle maker God has called you to be has the potential to literally change the world! So, get out there! Explore. Have vision. Be watchful of God's prompting. Focus on a passionate purpose you are trying to achieve. Stick to it. I promise, you will find other people who'll join you. You'll discover new and exciting opportunities you never imagined. Just stay flexible, and be ready and willing to course-correct if you start to get offtrack. God is leading you on a miraculous journey on which miracle will give way to miracle. He has the path laid out in front of you, and the results will be astounding.

Seventh Miracle Scroll

I Am God's Great Masterpiece

I am the love of God made visible.

I was conceived by the love of God

and brought forth to do wonders.

I am rare, and there is value in all rarity;

therefore, I am valuable and

forever increasing my value and worth.

I am a wonderfully unique creature of nature.

I am one of a kind.

There is no one else like me.

I am God's masterpiece.

8

Working Toward Miracles

Have you ever stopped to take a careful inventory of your life? If not, I challenge you to do so right now. Think about what God has placed in your care. Are you in good health? Have you been blessed with a close circle of friends and family? Do you receive any type of income? Is there a roof over your head? Go slowly and think through absolutely everything that God has entrusted to you; don't take any individual thing for granted. These can be physical, emotional, spiritual, relational, intellectual—anything goes!

What has God blessed you with? Ask God to help as you go through this exercise, and don't stop until you simply can't think of one more thing.

I talk to so many people who desperately want and need a miracle in their lives. They sit and they pray; they pray and they sit; they wait and wait and wait. Sometimes I just want to grab them by the shoulders and yell, "What are you waiting for? If you want a miracle, then get up and make something happen!"

I actually find this exercise exhausting, because I see everything in my life as a blessing in one way or another. I pray along with the psalmist, "Praise the LORD, my soul, and forget not all his benefits" (Psalm 103:2). If someone were to approach you and comment on what a wonderful life God has blessed you with, would your response be, "Yes, He has, and I'm grateful!"? You see, our life is not our own. God has given us everything—even our very life itself—to honor him and to be a blessing to others.

As you look over your list of blessings, never forget that they contain within them enormous opportunities for growth—both for ourselves and in the world around us. And so I ask you pointedly, *What are you doing with the blessings and opportunities God has placed at your feet?* I, for one, would like to turn these blessings into miracles! To do that, we must be mindful of the opportunities to bless others using the gifts God has put in our lives. And that, my friend, often requires us to get to work.

Opportunity Looks Like Work

I talk to so many people who desperately want and need a miracle in their lives. They sit and they pray; they pray and they sit; they wait and wait and wait. Sometimes I just want to grab them by the shoulders and yell, "What are you waiting for? If you want a miracle, then get up and make something happen!" We've said the phrase *miracle maker* often throughout this book, but let's stop and look at the key word in the term: *Maker* implies that we are actually *making* something happen! I can't name anything that was *made* simply by someone sitting around and waiting. *Making* requires action!

A farmer may be blessed with the most incredible crops that have ever been seen in all of history, but unless he actually harvests them, they're worthless. Our lives and the blessings we've received have been given to us by our heavenly

Father. If we want to see a rich crop of miracles flow through our lives, then we have to go about the task of tending the field and making the best of every opportunity God so graciously provides. In doing that, we provide an abundance not only for ourselves and our family, but an overflow to be shared with others. When that overflow spills out and impacts someone else's life in a dramatic, unexpected, and life-changing way, what word do you think they would use to describe it? They'd call it a miracle! And they'd be right.

We credit Thomas Edison with the invention of the first commercially practical lightbulb, but we hardly consider all that it took to literally create light in a bottle that would last for months. Do you think he had the idea for the lightbulb over breakfast and sat under its warm glow by lunch? Of course not! He worked at it for months and "failed" thousands of times—at least that's how others might have seen it. But when asked about it, the hard-working Edison replied, "I have not failed. I've just found 10,000 ways that won't work." That's because Edison was not confused about the connection between hard work and miraculous opportunities. He is well known for his other inspiring quotes on the virtue of hard work, such as, "Opportunity is missed by most people because it is dressed in overalls and looks like work" and "Everything comes to him who hustles while he waits."

That brings us back to our discussion about waiting for miracles. Yes, God can and will move in sudden, dramatic ways. We've said before that God is the "first cause," meaning He will move mountains at His own initiative. However, those are not the only miracles we experience in life. In fact, I'd argue that *most* of the miracles we see are those that require the active participation of a "second cause," which is a person who is willing to step into the flow of God's miracle-making current and make something happen.

Taking the First Step

The gospel story of Jesus walking on water is one of the most well-known recorded miracles. The image is so prevalent, in fact, that the phrase *he walks on water* has become a common term used to describe someone who is lucky. Truthfully, the image of Jesus walking atop a raging lake in the predawn hours is breathtaking. That certainly qualifies as a miracle! However, at least in Matthew's telling, Jesus wasn't the only man who took a stroll on the surface of the water that night. Take a look:

Immediately Jesus made the disciples get into the boat and go on ahead of him to the other side, while he dismissed the crowd. After he had dismissed them, he went up on a mountainside by himself to pray. Later that night, he was there alone, and the boat was already a considerable distance from land, buffeted by the waves because the wind was against it.

Shortly before dawn Jesus went out to them, walking on the lake. When the disciples saw him walking on the lake, they were terrified. "It's a ghost," they said, and cried out in fear.

But Jesus immediately said to them: "Take courage! It is I. Don't be afraid."

"Lord, if it's you," Peter replied, "tell me to come to you on the water."

"Come," he said.

Then Peter got down out of the boat, walked on the water and came toward Jesus. But when he saw the wind, he was afraid and, beginning to sink, cried out, "Lord, save me!"

Immediately Jesus reached out his hand and caught him. "You of little faith," he said, "why did you doubt?"

And when they climbed into the boat, the wind died down. Then those who were in the boat worshiped him, saying, "Truly you are the Son of God" (Matthew 14:22–33).

If we're not careful, we can read that passage too quickly and picture Peter simply jumping over the side of the boat without a thought. Do you think that's really how it happened? I tend to think there was at least a slight pause between Jesus' call and Peter's first step on the water. What must Peter have been thinking at that moment? The waves were crashing and the boat was rising and falling on the waters. Even if he had managed to sleep that night during the raging winds, he was no doubt groggy from the early predawn wake-up call. And let's not forget that his pulse is likely still racing from his initial fright that Jesus was actually a ghost! This was definitely not a calm, serene, or peaceful scene. This was not a "step of faith" that one takes alone while sitting safely on the sofa. No, this was an *actual* step of faith; a step that could have cost Peter his very life. And that required some careful thinking.

Yet, for whatever reason, Peter decided, "Yes, I can trust Jesus. Yes, I am willing to make this leap. Yes, it's time for me to put my faith to work and meet Jesus halfway." That's all

Jesus was waiting for. Sure, Jesus could have picked up Peter and forcibly thrown him out of the boat. If Jesus or Peter had acted differently, the gospels might have recorded the picture of Peter *landing*—rather than *stepping*—on the surface of the water! But what would that have cost us, even these thousands of years later? Did the miracle happen when Peter stood on the waves or when he lifted his leg over the side of the boat? I tend to believe that the miracle began when Peter made the decision to act.

One lesson we can learn from Peter that night is this: The safety of the boat allows us to only *see* miracles. If we want to *be* the miracle, we have to take action and lift our legs out of the safety of the boat.

That same principle is true in the miracles we participate in. The hard part is not watching God do amazing things. That may be the most exciting part, but honestly, that part is easy. I'm sure the disciples had a great show once they realized it was Jesus, not a ghost, who was defying natural laws by walking toward them on the water. How thrilling that must have been to see! But no, the hard part is when we have to face the inner struggles—the doubts and fears that want to keep us safe, warm, and dry in the boat. How many miracles are we missing because we're too scared (or lazy) to take that step of faith and action?

One lesson we can learn from Peter that night is this: The safety of the boat allows us to only *see* miracles. If we want to *be* the miracle, we have to take action, lift our legs out of the safety of the boat, and meet Jesus where He is.

It is perfectly acceptable to expect God to move in mighty ways, but He has still called us to prepare the fields. We cannot simply sit around and wait, hoping that He does something or sends someone to fix our problems. That's not how He operates. God does not work on our schedule or to our specifications. He has wired us to work toward goals, and as we work toward them, He will show up all throughout the process.

Eighth Miracle Scroll

I Have Unlimited Potential

I have unlimited potential

to think, grow, and develop.

Only I can choose what I want to manifest.

My potential hungers for my use.

I can and will vastly increase

my accomplishments a thousandfold

for the benefit of all.

9

Team Up to Make Miracles

Missie was terrified of one of life's greatest joys: a good night's sleep. For more than a decade, this bright, smiling twenty-five-year-old woman faced unimaginable demons and nightly torture. Intense nightmares had plagued her sleep almost every night since she was a young girl, and the years of sleepless fright had taken a tremendous toll. This was a burden she bore alone all that time, never telling anyone what was happening or sharing her concerns with friends or family. She was going into battle every single night as she pulled back the covers, but she was an army of one. She was losing.

This young lady was certainly a prayer warrior. She prayed and prayed over this issue, and yet her lonely prayers went unanswered. Missie was active in different prayer groups, as well, always laboring over the pain and struggles of those around her. Her magnificent prayers were like spontaneous songs of praise offered for the benefit of others. The friends in her prayer circle loved to hear her pray, and they all testified to the power in her prayers and the way God worked through her to bring blessings and miracles into their lives. She desperately wanted that kind of miracle in her own life, but she kept her deep need to herself for years.

While Jesus certainly seeks a relationship with every *individual* man, woman, and child, there is an undeniable power and presence of the Lord when a group of believers comes together.

Finally, one afternoon at work, Missie opened up about her nightmare problem to her prayer circle (one of the perks of working for a Christian ministry). Upon hearing her heartbreaking story, Missie's boss didn't hesitate. "Okay, Missie. We're going to deal with this right now." He moved an empty chair to the center of the room. "You sit here. Everyone else, gather around her. We have some work to do, and we're going to do this *together*."

The next twenty minutes were filled with prayer after prayer, offered in an unmatched loving intensity that Missie had never experienced. As each friend and partner prayed over her, Missie felt her burdens fall off her back like bricks. One by one, the group laid their hands on her and offered their petition to the Lord. They were focused. They were wholly unified in their mission and purpose. No one doubted; no one looked around the room; no one checked their watches or worried about missing a meeting or skipping lunch. Those assembled were acting in perfect unity, focusing their hearts, minds, and prayers on a single goal: to petition God to free this beautiful young woman from a decade of torment.

When the last amen went forth, Missie looked up weeping. "Thank you," she mouthed in a broken, emotional whisper. "Thank you." That night, Missie had the first peaceful night's sleep she'd had since she was a young child. Night after night from that point on, Missie experienced what others take for granted: rest. The nightmares were gone for good.

Where Two or Three Are Gathered

In Matthew 18:20, Jesus said, "For where two or three gather in my name, there am I with them." While Jesus certainly seeks a relationship with every *individual* man, woman, and child, there is an undeniable power and presence of the Lord when a group of believers comes together. In fact, Andrew Carnegie believed this cooperation is what facilitates miracles, and I agree. To become a miracle maker, you must have a magnificent obsession backed by a dedicated team. That's why, long ago, I composed an acrostic for TEAM:

Together

Everyone

Accomplishes

Miracles

Putting together two or more like-minded people with a clear intention can make your life, family, church, company, country, charity, or group hugely successful and effective. It's the beginning of your Dream Team, or what Carnegie called a Mastermind Alliance.

Andrew Carnegie was a Scottish immigrant who became America's richest man. He attributed his wealth not only to his reading of the Bible, but also to the fact that he learned to understand and actually apply its wisdom to his life and business. Carnegie's primary profession was the steel industry, although he had several other ventures throughout his life. His Mastermind Alliance consisted of approximately fifty men whom he brought together for the specific purpose of manufacturing and marketing steel. Carnegie credited his entire fortune to the power he accumulated through this "mastermind" experience.

Carnegie noticed in his reading of Scripture that Jesus performed most, if not all, of His recorded miracles only after He had assembled His twelve disciples working in harmony. The steel magnate saw this as a principle of cooperative teamwork that, if applied to his business, would empower him to build a great and thriving enterprise that would enrich not only his family and partners, but the country as a whole.

Inspired by Jesus' intentional, direct calling of each of the twelve disciples, Andrew Carnegie always had an eye out for potential team members. One day, he came across a day laborer that wanted to work diligently with Carnegie to create a great steel industry. The men were like-minded and focused in their efforts, and God richly blessed them as a result. His new partner's name was Charles Schwab—a man who went on to make quite a name for himself, as well. Together, Carnegie and Schwab built an unbeatable organization.

If you want to live up to your true miracle-making potential, you cannot operate alone. You need a team to work with you, pray with you, pick you up when you fall, applaud when you succeed, and push you forward when you stall.

Later in life, Andrew Carnegie granted a thorough, three-day interview to author Napoleon Hill. The entire interview is presented in Hill's book *How to Raise Your Salary*. In this masterwork, readers discover the principles and philosophy of how anyone anywhere can become infinitely more successful, happy, and accomplished. The first requirement is a dominating desire. The second is a mastermind team that believes intuitively in miracle-mindedness and miraculous achievements. Carnegie explained, "A mastermind team has two or more people working in the spirit of cooperative harmony."

The requirements, again, are desire and teamwork. With these two fundamental forces, we can accomplish almost anything. Carnegie wanted everyone to know, share, and use these principles. They work for everyone! If you master their application and use them enough, you can accomplish greatness—maybe even a miracle.

A Cord of Three Strands

When we partner up with like-minded individuals, we magnify our miracle-making potential. Teamwork creates exponential power. If one person can lift one hundred pounds, we should not assume that two people working together can lift only twice as much. Instead, the cooperative pair can lift much more than that *together*! Ecclesiastes 4:9 makes this point: "Two are better than one, because they have a good return for their labor." Beyond simply magnifying our efforts, however, working with a team provides an invaluable source of protection and encouragement. Ecclesiastes 4 continues, "If either of them falls down, one can help the other up. But pity anyone who falls and has no one to help them up. Also, if two lie down together, they will keep warm. But how can one keep warm alone? Though one may be overpowered, two can defend themselves. A cord of three strands is not quickly broken" (4:10–12).

If you want to live up to your true miracle-making potential, you cannot operate alone. You need a team to work with you, pray with you, pick you up when you fall, applaud when you succeed, and push you forward when you stall. I cannot be sure of the perfect number of like-minded associates you need, but here's a thought: Find twelve. That's certainly not a magic number, but it *is* the model demonstrated by Jesus. Twelve is just enough to provide ample support and variety of experiences and voices, but not so big as to create a slow-moving, disjointed committee. And be wise in your selections. You become like the people with whom you associate, so be sure the team members you choose demonstrate the fruit you'd like to see develop in your life.

What should you do in your group meetings? That is up to you and God. However, especially as you get started and as you carry on through your years together, never lose sight of the power of prayer. Praying together keeps the focus of your enterprise where it must always remain: the God who works in, through, and around you. Your miracles are not your own; they flow through you from the Father. It is He who will bring your mastermind group together, and it is He who will work miracles among you.

Ninth Miracle Scroll

My Tomorrows Are Extraordinary

The miracle of my birth was a great beginning,

and with God I will extend my miracles daily.

Every day I am passionately on purpose

to do great work, and it excites me to do so.

I will set great and inspiring goals and work

to achieve them.

I will create more and more goals

as destinations for my future achievements.

I will fulfill my potential to its limits.

I will constantly and continually improve my

thinking, language, vocabulary, etiquette,

graces, politeness, and personal skills.

I will be love made visible.

10

Be the Miracle You Never Know About

Deborah Rosado Shaw was a hard-working single mom with three little kids. One day, while shopping at her local Target store, her mind was wildly distracted with all the stress in her life. She was worried about her kids and worried about how to provide for them. She had big goals in life, but she was having a hard time getting traction. As she pushed her cart up and down the aisles that day, she found herself thinking the same thing over and over again: *I need a miracle.*

With that thought running through her mind, she found herself absentmindedly walking through the book section of the store. Three times, she passed by my book *The Aladdin Factor*. Three times, it fell off the shelf at her feet. Three times, she picked it up and put it back. After the third time, she came to her senses and wondered if this could be the miracle she was hoping for. Maybe it was! She decided to buy the book with the little money she had in her purse, and she started reading it as soon as she got home.

She had a lightbulb moment when she read, "The right question gives you the answer. There is always a profitable way to improve the value of every product, service, information, personality, or idea." Deborah was in the business of selling umbrellas. Following the book's advice, she set her mind to dreaming of new innovations in the area of umbrellas. What could she do that had never been done with something so common?

Voila! An idea struck her like a lightning bolt. What's the most annoying thing about walking with an umbrella at night? It's trying to see where you're going when it's dark and raining! And, since your hands are already at least partially full with the umbrella itself, it's a terrible nuisance to *also* carry a flashlight to light your path. So, what if Deborah could devise an elegant solution for integrating a flashlight *into* the handle of an umbrella? She got to work on her idea, and soon the first units were rolling off the production line. The public's response was overwhelming! They loved them! She had customers ready to buy the umbrellas as fast as she could make them. People were buying two or three for themselves and buying even more for gifts. She had struck gold! Best of all, Deborah created, owned, and operated the business all on her own, and she made her first fortune soon after when she decided to sell her umbrella-flashlight business.

This was all especially exciting for a once-struggling single mom from humble inner-city beginnings. Over time, Deb emerged as an entrepreneurial superstar and role model. She built and sold a multimillion-dollar international merchandising company, and her business expertise enabled her to negotiate and close deals with the smartest buyers in the world at Costco, Walmart, Toys"R"Us, and even the Walt Disney Company. She has served on the boards of PepsiCo, Walmart, and many more. She advises the leadership of great companies on how they can sell, serve, and help the fifty million Hispanics in America. And as a world-class speaker, Deb is a powerhouse who tells audiences everywhere that they are unique in the world and have the ability to choose success for themselves.

We May Never Know

Deborah Rosado Shaw's life is a miracle through and through, and that particular string of miracles started with my little book, *The Aladdin Factor*, mysteriously falling off the shelf at her feet several times. I cannot tell you how grateful I am to know that story and to have had the pleasure of spending time with Deb in the years since that fateful day when her shopping trip was miraculously interrupted.

As I think about our discussion of miracles and about Deb's story in particular, something incredibly humbling stands out to me: All of these wonderful things happened in Deborah's life before I ever knew her. God used my book to start a magnificent string of miracles that completely changed her life and her family legacy forever, and I might never have known. Of course, I've now had the privilege of getting to know Deb, but the truth is, I will never know all the different ways God has used—and will continue to use—me in working miracles in the lives of others. The same is true, of course, of your miracles.

That is such a critical piece of the miracle-making puzzle, but it is one we so often miss. We can get so focused on blessing the people in our immediate circle that we become totally blind to how God may use us in ways we never even know about.

We can get so focused on blessing the people in our immediate circle that we become totally blind to how God may use us in ways we never even know about.

As an author, this is one of the most exciting parts of the miracle-making discussion. I am enormously blessed to know many of the miracle stories that have come about through my work, but I realize I will only ever know the smallest fraction of what God has done and will do through my books. This brings me to one of the greatest joys and challenges in the life of a miracle maker: God will continue to work miracles in and through us that we never even know about.

Beginning Our Big Miracle

To emphasize this point, I'd like to tell you a little of the behind-the-scenes history involved in my best-selling book series, Chicken Soup for the Soul. Perhaps hearing some of the stories we have heard will help you get a vision for how powerfully God continues to work through all of our lives, even when we don't know how, when, why, or for whom He's pouring out His miracles.

Back in the early nineties, Jack Canfield and I felt a terrible burden for the American people. We grew more and more convinced that we as a nation, and even the people of the world as a whole, were emotionally debilitated and in need of spiritual and emotional healing. As a natural storyteller, it was my strong belief that nothing changes people's mood, and therefore their behavior, as well as a good story. As Jack and I talked, we felt a strong conviction that we were supposed to help the nation get back on track by collecting the most encouraging, powerful stories we could find and putting them in the hands of as many people as possible. That's how the *Chicken Soup for the Soul* idea was born.

For three years, Jack and I worked together to make our dream a reality. Every single day during that time, we felt as though we were living and breathing this grand vision God had put on our hearts. That purposeful spirit is what kept us going throughout the long and sometimes grueling process.

It also kept us motivated and excited in the face of one adversity and disappointment after another.

Looking back more than twenty years later, it may seem as though the book was an obvious hit from the start. At the time, though, we had a hard time convincing anyone to even publish it! We lived through 144 individual rejections. It seemed as though every day someone was telling us no. We got to where we'd just laugh and turn their answer around. Instead of reading "no," we read it as "on," as though a seemingly endless stream of publishers was calling us "onward, boys!" We knew in our souls that we had a big winner, a best-selling book series. We knew without a doubt that God had put this vision in our hearts and that He had big plans for what He wanted to accomplish through our work. So, no matter what our critics, relatives, naysayers, or would-be publishers told us, we just kept moving forward.

We owned, wrote, and believed in an outrageous outcome, even when there was no obvious reason to do so. That's the spirit of making miracles; we had a call on our hearts to do something, and we were going to do it. In that spirit, we wrote what we called a "Wow of a Business Plan" for the series we had envisioned. Our first written goal was to sell 1.5 million books in a year and a half—and from June 28, 1993, through Christmas Day of 1994, we sold 1.3 million books. We came up two hundred thousand copies short of our goal. Was that a failure? Of course not! We were doing what no one thought we could do, and God was pushing us forward with more momentum than we had ever imagined! It was a miracle in the making!

At that point, we set another goal to sell five million books in 1995. We made it! And then, by 2000, we were selling fifteen million books a year. Now, twenty years later, we have sold half a billion books—well on our way to our big-vision goal: selling one billion books. The only book in history to sell more than a billion copies is the Bible, and people kept telling me, "You can't outsell the Bible!" I took that as a challenge, not because I wanted to outsell the Bible, but because I believe in giant, miracle-sized goals.

In the spirit of making miracles, I decided that I didn't have to start from scratch to reach that goal; I could look at what God is already doing and join Him there. So, I worked to create a customized edition of the Good Book that would appeal to millions of people who wouldn't normally pick up a traditional black leather Bible with gold trim. The *Chicken Soup for the Soul Bible* was a huge hit! It was unintimidating with a lovely purple cover and little "chicken soupy" stories to bring new life and perspective to the Word that was comfortable for those who weren't used to reading the Scriptures. At its peak, our Bible edition was selling seventy thousand copies a week at Walmart. Readers loved it, shared it, talked about it, and made it a colossal bestseller. People were reading the Bible for the first time; it was a miracle, and it was all because some well-meaning critic had said, "You can't outsell the Bible." All that challenge did was make me find a new way to make a miracle to serve those who weren't being served. Again, that's what you do when you're operating with the miracle mindset: you make a way to do the impossible.

Miraculous Results

With some of that history out of the way, let's look at ways God worked through our little books to bring miracles to other people—some whom we knew, and others we had never met and might never have met at all.

I said we received 144 rejections from publishers. The publisher who finally caught our vision for the book, Peter Vegso of HCI Books, was one of the first to realize a miracle. When we first joined up with him, HCI was on the verge of bankruptcy with $17 million in debts they couldn't pay.

However, Peter fought alongside us in those early days, and as a result, our success became his success. At our sales zenith of fifteen million books per year, our publisher had three different shifts of 168 printers each working around the clock to produce enough books to meet that outrageous demand. Peter, the team at HCI, the multiple shifts of printers, and many more had experienced a miracle because just a few years earlier, they expected to be out of work. But now, they were riding high with success they'd never imagined. God had used Jack and me to do something unbelievable and unexpected for those fine men and women, and we were blessed right alongside them.

That blessing passed right down through the booksellers too. The 4,700 independent bookstores—called "indies" by the American Booksellers Association (ABA)—often came up to us at the annual meetings with tears in their eyes. They hugged us and said, "Your book series got people to come back into our store and saved us from bankruptcy!" One couple said it plainly, "You were the miracle that I had been praying for." I love hearing those words!

Perhaps the most moving story I've heard came as Jack and I signed books at an annual ABA convention. We had eight hundred people waiting in line to get a free copy of an as-yet-unreleased *Chicken Soup* book. The ABA normally limits an author's signings to one hour, but the fastest we could possibly go was five hundred books in an hour. We had already promised books and signatures to everyone in line, so we knew we were going to be there a while. It was going to be a long afternoon.

During this frantic signing, while I was doing my best to keep up with the endless line of chatty fans, Jack leaned over and whispered, "Stop signing. You need to hear this." I looked up and saw that my friend had tears in his eyes. That wasn't uncommon, as we often heard deeply touching, personal stories from people at our book signings.

The man standing before us said, "You saved my country!" Of all the things I had heard from kind people over the years, that was a first! He continued, "I am a Lebanese university professor. Every night I have to convince thousands of my people to keep Lebanon free from Syrian invasion. I asked my people to risk their life and limbs to defend our great country. I shared your *Chicken Soup* stories every night to inspire them to stay the course and keep our country safe. I have with me a man who wants to personally thank you. He listened and believed. He fought bravely and valiantly. In his efforts, he had both of his arms shot off."

The professor's friend stepped forward and we saw that both sleeves of his suit coat had been cut off and sewed together at the shoulders. He had a wonderful smile that shined as he said, "Your great stories helped save my country. Most importantly, they gave me hope. They still do. I came 5,620 miles with my teacher, friend, and mentor to thank you personally for what you have done for Lebanon." At this point, all of us had tears streaming down our faces. We hugged the man and he kissed our cheeks. It was a beautiful moment that I will never forget. It is truly remarkable what kind of miracles God brings about when we simply seek to make miracles whenever and however we can.

The Miracles You Never Know

These stories warm my spirit and leave me practically speechless. When I stop and think about the miracles God's brought about in, through, and around me, all I can do is throw up my arms and pray with the apostle Paul, "Oh, the depth of the riches of the wisdom and knowledge of God! How unsearchable his judgments, and his paths beyond tracing out!" (Romans 11:33). The truth is, Jack and I will never know but a slim sliver of the miraculous stories that have come about through our work. The few stories I know are absolutely mind blowing, but I'm sure the greatest ones are most likely the ones I'll never hear.

When I stop and think about the miracles God's brought about in, through, and around me, all I can do is throw up my arms and pray with the apostle Paul, "Oh, the depth of the riches of the wisdom and knowledge of God!"

That may seem sad to some, but not to me. In fact, it is one of the greatest encouragements of my career. To think that God can use the work I do, sitting right here at this computer keyboard, to impact untold millions of people around the world, is nothing short of miraculous. But you don't need a best-selling book to impact hundreds or thousands or even millions of people you'll never meet. That's the call God's placed on my life; it doesn't have to be the call He's put on yours. Everyone is uniquely gifted to make a specific impact on the world. You cannot compare your miracles to anyone else's. Your miracles are your own, and each one is a precious gift from God for a precise purpose. You can and will be a miracle to others—certainly to those you can see, hear, and talk to, but perhaps even more so to the ones you can't.

Tenth Miracle Scroll

I Will Survive and Thrive

I will delight in challenges

because I know that with God

I can resolve every crisis.

I will survive and thrive.

Problems are opportunities in disguise.

They are here to inspire my growth

and help me discover creative solutions.

Obstacles before me are there to be overcome.

I will use all my talents and resources to solve them

because I am certain of God's desire

to have me survive and thrive.

11

Making Miracles
for a Living

I have a confession to make, and you probably won't believe me. You know by now that I've been blessed with the opportunity to speak professionally for a few decades. You've read about how I had to hustle to get those opportunities going in the early days. And you know that I've put a lot of time and energy into writing and selling books—and God has certainly blessed that effort! I have traveled all over the world; I have lugged suitcases on and off airplanes more times than I can count; and I have run from one engagement to another in all-out sprints down busy sidewalks. I have poured my blood, sweat, and tears into my career every day of my adult life. And it all started six months after going through bankruptcy, feeling trashed and washed up. That's when I, along with sixteen others, was invited by my professional speaking mentor, Cavett Robert, to attend the first meeting of the National Speakers Association (NSA). At the meeting he said, "It's not how big a piece of the pie we get; it's how big we can make the pie for everyone."

Most speakers in 1974 were either pros working for the likes of General Motors or Ford Motor Company, such as Dr. Ken McFarlane and Bill Gove, earning what seemed at the time enormous fees of one thousand dollars per talk and doing a hundred engagements a year. Cavett, though, spoke whenever and wherever opportunities arose—five hundred times a year for five hundred dollars per speech or seminar. He was also the first ever to sell information products from the stage, earning over ten times as much.

Other professional speakers back then criticized Cavett for polluting a profession and bringing in too much competition. But Cavett thought everyone should learn to speak, and he believed the more speakers there are the more truth and inspiration spreads when attendees bring leaders' messages home and "brand them into their brains and etch them into the fabric of their very being and then share them with colleagues, families, and friends to make everyone better off." Thanks to Cavett's big heart and brilliance, today there are more than five thousand members of NSA and more than twelve thousand professional speakers around the world working to make the pie bigger and better for all people.

Regardless of your career path or the title after your name, you also can make miracles for a living, experiencing every day as an adventure and a gift from God. I guarantee you'll love every minute of it and, like me, feel as if you'll *never work another day in your life*!

In a talk that was inspired by Will Rogers' speech titled "You Can't Heat an Oven with Snowballs," Cavett said in his Mississippi drawl, "Speaking ain't work if you love it. You will never work another day in your life if you love what you're doing as much as I love what I am doing, speaking to inspire you to fulfill your God-given destiny!" I couldn't agree more with that philosophy, which has become my lifeblood of everything I do.

I love speaking and writing, and my profession loves me. It has poured many, many miracles into my life. I want the same or more for you, my dear reader. No, it won't always be easy, but when you live from your passions, when you spend all day every day making miracles and watching people's lives change right in front of you, it's hard to call it "work." Regardless of your career path or the title after your name, you also can make miracles for a living, experiencing every day as an adventure and a gift from God. I guarantee you'll love every minute of it and, like me, feel as if you'll *never work another day in your life*!

Giving the Miracle of Hearing

I can hear again! It's amazing. I didn't know what I was missing. I can hear my beautiful wife whisper that she loves me without having to read her lips. I can hear my feet and the noise they make crumpling carpet fibers. I can hear the rustle of the wind and the sweet ringing of the chimes being blown on my patio. I can hear the full orchestration of church bells on Sunday morning, and I can understand every word that the worshipers are singing. I am rejoicing in the cacophony of miraculous sounds!

For so many years, without knowing it, I was missing

90 percent of certain high ranges that normal listeners hear. I didn't even know they were available to enjoy! Noises like a whistling teakettle or the screeching of my accidentally tripped home alarm were completely outside my hearing—but not any longer! Now, with the aid of modern technology, I have the full gift of hearing again, and it is miraculous!

Getting my hearing aid opened more than my ears; it opened my eyes to a whole community of people in desperate need of a miracle. Losing only some of my hearing and experiencing the joy of having it restored put a burden on my heart for those who have lost most or all of their ability to hear. That's why I am so excited about the work my friends Bill and Tanni Austin are doing for the world's deaf population.

The Starkey Hearing Foundation, led by the Austins, is a humanitarian organization committed to doing whatever it takes to bring the miracle of hearing to whoever needs it, anywhere in the world. Bill privately owns the largest hearing technology company in the world. At seventy-three years old, Bill has spent more than half a century becoming the Picasso of the hearing aid field. And yet, despite his great business success, Bill's always been most motivated by helping those in need. For him, it's not just about giving people the ability to hear; it's about giving people dignity and self-respect. That's why he spends 99 perent of his time working with the foundation. He has to; at the 2010 Clinton Global Initiative, he promised former President Bill Clinton that he would give away one million hearing aids in a decade! It's a giant goal, but as of late 2014, the foundation is 40 percent ahead of schedule! Bill Austin simply cannot be stopped in his crusade to spread the miracle of hearing.

Children are a special concern of the Starkey Foundation. Bill told me, "If children do not get to hear before four years old, it becomes very difficult for them to learn to speak and vocalize." This is especially true in some of the poorest communities on earth, where the foundation supplies free hearing aids and a full supply of extra batteries. Through their work, some of the weakest members of these communities now have a good chance at literacy and ending the poverty cycle. Bill and the foundation are doing everything they can to get to these children around the world in time.

Bill's generosity doesn't just extend to the poorest countries around the world. It actually starts at home, right in the heart of his thriving hearing aid business. He runs the biggest hearing aid manufacturing company in America. He is known far and wide as a master in the field. He could likely charge anything he wants for his world-class products, but the method of payment that excites him most is "fund." Bill has always told his entire team that if individuals cannot afford to pay for their hearing aid, they are required to write the word *FUND* on the order and let those customers have their hearing aid at no cost. His credo is, "Alone we can do so little, but together we can change the world!"

Bill Austin is an incredible man, and I have been blessed to spend time with him several times throughout the years. We first met when we both attended an entrepreneurship meeting at Richard Branson's Necker Island several years ago. He described himself as the "master of hearing," the man who had outfitted everyone in need of hearing assistance from Presidents Reagan, Clinton, and Bush (both) and Mother Teresa, Elton John, Pope John Paul II, and Billy Graham. His facility is affectionately known as the Mayo Clinic of Hearing. There is no question that Bill Austin is a hardworking entrepreneur and world-renowned expert in his field. He could do absolutely anything he wanted to do with his time, but his favorite thing in the world to do is to make miracles for men, women, and children who are all-too-often overlooked. He could never be content simply going to a *job*, putting in his mandatory eight hours, and then going home. Impossible! Never settling for simply "making hearing aids," Bill would probably say his chief job is to give the miracle of hearing to those in need. He has turned his career into his life's calling, and he'll leave more than a million miracles behind him before he's done.

Giving for a Living

Brad Formsma is another fantastic example of someone who's figured out how to turn his full-time career into a string of beautiful miracles. However, Brad's situation is a little different: He doesn't just *make* miracles; he *collects* them.

Brad started cutting yards while in high school, and that venture grew over the years, one yard at a time, into a full-fledged landscaping business after college. He added construction and heavy equipment to his company's list of services, and it became surprisingly successful. He and his wife, Laura, enjoyed the money they were making. He admits, "We became really good at giving to ourselves while giving just a little to others." Having grown up in the church, Brad saw giving as an ideal, but it wasn't a big motivator in his life at the time. He was after what he thought made people successful: money, position, and prestige.

That climb up the ladder took a sharp turn the day Brad prayed a dangerous prayer. He and his wife had been wrestling with how to make their faith a bigger part of their lives, and Brad eventually prayed, "Wherever You are, take over my life, and I'll do what You want me to do." That's when things started to change. That prayer—plus a couple of sour business deals that dealt Brad a humbling blow—changed Brad's heart over the next few years. The family started dabbling in giving, first by writing a check to a charity organization, then by helping needy people pay for their groceries in the checkout line, then by finding bigger and more dramatic ways to give.

All this time, Brad's business continued to grow, but it wasn't his business accomplishments that made him feel successful; it was his experiments in generosity. He was becoming more and more addicted to the joy he experienced when God used him to bring a miracle into another family's life. Then, the critical moment came. Someone posed a challenging question to Brad, and his answer surprised him. When asked what his absolute dream job would be, Brad replied, "I would love to encourage people in their giving because I believe we live in a self-focused world, and that conflicts with my belief that it is more blessed to give than to receive." That answer would change the course of Brad's life over the next few years.

Brad began volunteering with a nonprofit organization called Generous Giving. It wasn't long, though, before he dove in with both feet by selling his successful landscaping businesses and going to work for the nonprofit full-time. While he found the strategic and planning work of the nonprofit important, he never felt fully satisfied focusing only on the big picture of giving. He liked to hear stories about specific moments when God used someone to change another person's life. He wanted to hear about the miracles.

For example, Brad loves to tell the story of how he and his family blessed a refugee family in their city. The struggling Sudanese family, who depended on bicycles as their main mode of transportation, had had their bikes stolen. The local Sunday paper ran a short story about it one weekend, and it sparked something in Brad's heart. He asked his young son what he thought they should do to help these strangers, and the boy didn't hesitate: "We should buy them bikes!" he exclaimed. Of course, Brad agreed and the whole family piled into the van for a day of miracles.

After purchasing bicycles for the refugee family, the Formsmas drove to the area mentioned in the newspaper and looked for the house pictured in the article. After waiting several hours for the family to get home, Brad, his wife, and their two children excitedly rang the doorbell and unloaded the gifts. The unsuspecting family was shocked! Through broken English and a huge smile, all the grateful father could say was, "I like bike! I like bike!"[4]

That story was repeated so often and to so many groups of people that it sparked an "I Like" revolution! Brad began receiving more and more "I Like" stories that told of specific, meaningful ways people were going outside their comfort zones and doing something significant for someone else. Brad partnered with a friend who was a film producer to put some of these touching stories on film. These short videos became so popular and widely distributed that Brad left Generous Giving and started his own nonprofit organization appropriately named I Like Giving.

Through his new nonprofit, their short films, and their popular website, ILikeGiving.com (where you can see the "I Like Bike" video), Brad Formsma is giving everyday miracle makers a place to share their stories. As more videos are circulated, more people are inspired to give, which results in more stories, and the cycle of giving continues. As a result, Brad now gets to experience something I've enjoyed for decades: a near-endless supply of powerful, inspirational stories of God working through people to change lives. A gifted entrepreneur, Brad could have continued to grow his landscaping business while he dabbled in generosity or he could have turned his giving-video idea into a new business venture, but that wasn't his motivation. He explains, "We could go out and do a lot in private business, but I believe we can do a much greater good if we do it the way we are." Brad's found a way to make miracles for a living, and he couldn't be happier.

Make Your Career Miraculous

One of the biggest blessings of my life has been the opportunity to spend my days teaching, coaching, and inspiring other people. It is an unbelievably infectious feeling to play some small part in what they see as miracles. To actually get paid while I do that, and to have the freedom and ability to do that all day every day, is a miracle unto itself!

However, you don't have to write books or go on the speaking circuit like me. There is something you can do in your career *today* to bring a miracle into someone's life. I don't care what you do for a living; I promise there is some way you can make a difference by blessing someone around you. Too many people think that the only way to win in business is to "look out for number one." That's a lie! Like the great Brian Tracey says, "Successful people are always looking for opportunities to help others. Unsuccessful people are always asking, 'What's in it for me?'" If you want to be a success, you must look for ways to bring miracles into someone else's life. As you help others win, you'll win too.

If you want to be a success, you must look for ways to bring miracles into someone else's life. As you help others win, you'll win too.

Become a Miracle Making Factor and Factory

Sometimes when you stimulate miracles, you don't hear about them and their effects on others until much later. I am super blessed to have deep friendships with many wonderful, powerful, and exceedingly successful people whom I love, trust, respect, and admire. I have known Trudy Green and her kids for years. They are great friends. Trudy has managed major rock stars like the Rolling Stones, Janet Jackson, Aerosmith, and multiple others. Her son, Ben Rolnik, is an uber bright young man who emanates persuasive brilliance.

Ben has extraordinary talents that I have attempted to hire into my company on several occasions. Ben knows many young and successful movers and shakers, literally around the world.

Recently, Ben called and said, "Mark, you have got to meet your best student ever. He was one of the early hires at Facebook, went to Harvard, and is building a world-changing business because he heard you speak in 1997 at a meeting at Ball State University before twenty thousand student leaders. His name is Chris Pan. Because of your dynamic and inspiring speech, he decided to become a speaker like you. Now, he wants to come to your office and thank you for inspiring him to greatness. Will you meet him?"

Chris Pan, thirty-seven years old, came to my office effusing his profound gratitude. He said, "I loved your powerful, inspirational, and insightful speech. I became a speaker because of you. Speaking helped me get into Harvard, and it started my early career at Facebook, where I was able to personally teach Mark Zuckerberg Chinese. That all happened because I was a highly visible speaker for the company."

Currently he is building The MyIntent Project—What's Your World? (www.myintent.org), where their mission is to be a catalyst for meaningful conversations and positive energy. They ask people to pick one word that they want as a daily reminder of their intent, and then Chris' organization sends them a bracelet with that word hand-engraved into it.

"My intent is for each bracelet to become the best, original, and immediate conversation starters ever," Chris enthused. "Everyone who gets one can't stop talking about it, and it's going viral. You launched a lot of miracles in my life. You are a miracle-generating factory, Mark, and I want to do the same in my lifetime. I love the idea that each MyIntent bracelet/word is a miracle!"

You are a miracle-generating factory too. So look for them in your life and I'm certain you'll see many more miracles happening in your life, in the lives of those around you, and be sure that miracles are happening even for people you may never meet.

Eleventh Miracle Scroll

I Am the Love That Creates Miracles

My heart is full of love,

which is the true miracle-making power.

I can forge love-creating miracles in my mind.

I can create miracles that create more miracles.

Because the secret of secrets is that

miracles are forged by love.

12

The Miracle
Question

We have talked so much about miracles in this book. We've discussed what they are and how they work. We've talked about huge cosmic miracles and simple, little ways a miracle changes the course of someone's life. We've talked about how to see the miracles in your own life, and we've seen several examples of how we can be the miracle in someone else's life. But here's where theory and encouragement become reality. This is where I hit you with a truth that will bring your miracle-making journey to an end—or set it into explosive motion. That truth is simply: none of this matters if you don't actually decide right now to become a miracle maker in the world.

I want to motivate you to change your life. If I can play some small role in God redirecting your life into a limitless string of miracles, then I will have the joy of participating in all those miracles with you. And you can do the same when you inspire others!

All of the talk and stories and theories in the world won't matter if they don't actually move you into action. You see, one of my hidden goals for this book has been to actually make a miracle *for you*. I want to motivate you to change your life. If I can play some small role in God redirecting your life into a limitless string of miracles, then I will have the joy of participating in all those miracles with you. And you can do the same when you inspire others! That's one of the many joys of this whole process; together, we can experience and participate in an exponential number of miracles! But that only happens when we dare to ask ourselves what I call "The Miracle Question." We'll find that life-changing question in the powerful story of John O'Leary.

The Power of One

In the late 1980s, John O'Leary was a typical nine-year-old boy growing up in St. Louis, Missouri. He had a good life with brothers and sisters, and with two wonderful parents who deeply loved each other and their kids. Life was good in the O'Leary family—until everything fell apart one Saturday morning.

Like any boy his age, John was fascinated by what he saw older boys doing. Earlier that week, John had watched as some older kids played with fire. They would light a small fire on the ground, back up a couple of feet, and then throw a little gasoline onto the flame to watch it explode to life. The spectacle was stuck in John's mind for days until the day he decided to give it a try himself. While his parents were away, John went into the garage and lit a small piece of cardboard on fire. His dad kept a five-gallon drum of gasoline in the garage, so John thought he'd pick up the whole can and drip just a little gas onto the fire to watch it spark. Now, this drum of gas actually weighed more than forty pounds, so the little boy had to pick it up in a bear hug and tip it ever so slightly over the open flame.

What the unsuspecting child didn't anticipate were the gas fumes that came out of the drum first. The invisible vapors ignited and immediately carried the flame into the full drum of gasoline. The can John was holding to his chest exploded, covering the boy with flaming gasoline and throwing him fifteen feet across the room. Still conscious and in a wild panic, John didn't stop, drop, and roll. Instead, he ran— through the flames, through the garage door into the kitchen, and through the family room—all while screaming for someone to help him. His seventeen-year-old brother, Jim, came running and, at the sight of his little brother standing in the foyer in flames, sprung into action. Jim grabbed a floor mat and started beating the flames out. For two and a half minutes, the older boy did all he could to rescue John. Finally, the flames were down enough for Jim to wrap up John, take him outside, and roll him in the grass to totally put the fire out.

When John arrived at the hospital, the doctors and nurses were surprised he was still alive. He had burns on 100 percent of his body; 87 percent of them were third-degree burns. He lay in the hospital bed fighting for his life as the medical team worked. His parents finally arrived and brought him some encouragement, but John cut through their encouraging words with a grim question: "Mama, am I going to die?"

Gathering all the strength she could, and knowing her answer would set the tone for the whole journey they were about to start, John's mother looked at him and asked, "John, do you want to die? Because it's your choice, not mine." He said no. She replied, "Then you've got to take the hand of God, walk together with Him, and you've got to fight like never before." With that, John and his family made the commitment to fight—although they had no idea what that would entail.

Soon, John was plunged into darkness. To prevent him from accidentally hurting himself, John was physically restrained in his bed, with his arms strapped to the rails. His lungs were badly burned, which meant breathing was extremely difficult. To make it easier, the doctors performed a tracheotomy, a procedure in which they cut a hole in John's throat to allow him to breath through a tube. This made breathing easier, but it meant that John was incapable of speaking. And, as his body swelled from the terrible injuries, the boy's eyes also swelled shut. So there he was, nine years old and fighting for his life, tied down to his bed, unable to speak, and in total darkness. All seemed lost—until a voice John knew well pierced his darkness.

John had grown up listening to baseball games on the radio every night throughout the summer, and there was one voice that every midwestern baseball fan knew well during those years. Hall of Fame announcer Jack Buck's deep, rough voice was deeply implanted into John's mind. As John explained it, "He's the guy who rocked me to sleep every night during the summertime as I was listening to his voice on the radio."

So, there's John, now lying in his hospital bed and terrified. He recalls, "I'm stretched out in the darkness, burned on a Saturday and now it's Sunday morning. The door opens up from the outside. I hear footsteps. Somebody walks in, they sit down, and they pull the chair up close. And then I hear this voice: 'Kid. Kid, wake up. You are going to live. You got that? You are going to survive. And when you get out of here, we are going to celebrate. We'll call it John O'Leary Day at the ballpark. Kid, are you listening?'" John nodded in agreement, unable to speak. That voice was unmistakable. It was the same voice that thrilled John on the radio all summer long. The legendary Jack Buck had just told John that he was going to live, and that boy's life was immediately filled with hope.

What John couldn't know was that his hero could only stay in the room with him for less than a minute that day because he didn't want John to hear him cry. Once Jack reached the safety of the hallway, he burst into tears. A nurse asked him if he was okay, and Jack replied, "I'm not sure. That little boy in room 406 . . . He's not going to make it, is he?"

The nurse lovingly looked him in the eye and told him the truth: "Mr. Buck, there is absolutely no chance. There's just nothing we can do. It's his time."

In thinking about that exchange years later, John said, "We all get that news at one time or another, whether it's in our business or our health or our relationships. And how we respond to that news matters. Jack Buck took that news home. He cried about it. He prayed about it. And then he asked a question. It's a simple question, but it's one I think we miss sometimes. The question he asked that night is: *What more can I do?*"

The next day, John was still tied to his bed in darkness. Again, he heard the door open and someone pull up a chair to his bed. Then he head that voice again, saying, "Kid, wake up. I'm back. You are going to live. You got that? You are going to survive. Keep fighting, because John O'Leary Day at the ballpark will make it all worthwhile."

For the next five months, Jack Buck journeyed with the little boy who was inspired to fight on. John recalled, "This man's life changed mine. It gave me something to believe in during a very, very difficult time. And together we raced forward, pushing toward possibility." Days turned into weeks and weeks turned into months. Finally, John was released from the hospital and he, Jack, and several thousand baseball fans enjoyed John O'Leary Day at the ballpark. It was a celebration! But even that was just one of many milestones ahead of John. The next big challenge was restoring some dignity to the young man.

As the months rolled on, John still had not returned to school. Before he could do that, he had to learn how to write again. This was a seemingly insurmountable challenge to the boy because he had no fingers left on either hand. His parents had tried to motivate him to write, but he was feeling too defeated to give it a good try. Jack Buck heard about this, and so again, he asked himself that question, *What more can I do?* And then the answer came.

A few days later, John received a package in the mail from Jack. It was a baseball signed by baseball great Ozzie Smith. The ball came with a note that simply said, "Kid, if you want a second baseball, all you have to do is handwrite a thank-you letter to the man who signed the first one."

The only problem was that John couldn't write. Jack knew this, of course, but he was trying to give John the motivation to make the effort. That night, John's parents held the pen in his hand and helped him scratch out an illegible thank-you note to Ozzie Smith. No one could probably read a word of it, but it was good enough to get John a second baseball signed by another famous baseball player. This one also came with a note: "Kid, if you want a third baseball, all you have to do is write another thank-you letter."

John recalls, "It was on. You ever notice how if you can do something once, it's way easier to do a second time?" And so John wrote another letter. A few days later, a third baseball arrived with the same note from Jack. This went on all summer. Before they were done, Jack had sent a total of sixty baseballs to John, who was now able to write perfectly legible thank-you notes all on his own. Jack's motivation worked! That persistence got John back into grade school, followed by high school, and ultimately through college. But Jack's string of miracles wasn't done yet.

The night of college graduation, John was surprised by a visit from his old friend and mentor. Jack showed up with a package for the boy he had walked with for more than a decade. Like all of Jack's packages, this one came with a note: "Kid, this means a lot to me. I hope it means a lot to you too. Enjoy. It's yours." John opened the box and found his sixty-first baseball, but there was something different about this one. The lights in the room were turned down low so John couldn't exactly make out what he was looking at. He took the box out to the hallway where the lights were brighter, and that's when he realized what Jack had given him. It was a beautiful baseball replica made entirely out of crystal, bearing this inscription:

Jack Buck

Baseball Hall of Fame

1987

It was the crystal baseball Jack had received when he was inducted into the Baseball Hall of Fame. It was priceless, not only for its value to the game of baseball. It was priceless because it symbolized the unbelievable power of one man to change someone else's life by daring to ask the often-impossible question, *What more can I do?*

Today, John is a healthy, happily married man raising four beautiful children. He is living his life's passion as a popular speaker who brings a strong message of hope and motivation to audiences all over the country. Through his appropriately titled speaking and leadership business, Rising Above, John O'Leary encourages people to push beyond their limits and past any obstacles by challenging them with Jack's simple question: *What more can I do?* None of this would have happened if, twenty-five years earlier while lying on a hospital bed, John had not heard the voice of a true miracle maker calling out to him, "Kid, wake up. You are going to live. You got that?"

In looking back, John said, "The miracle is love. The miracle is showing up for others because you care more about their life than you care about yourself. That's when the real miracle shows up."

In looking back, John said, "The miracle is love. The miracle is showing up for others because you care more about their life than you care about yourself. That's when the real miracle shows up."

I don't know anyone who is happier to be alive than John O'Leary. He is living miracle to miracle and encouraging thousands around the country to be miracle makers, just like his mentor, Jack Buck.

If you want to know more about him, visit his Web site, RisingAbove.com, and look for his upcoming book.

What More Can I Do?

Each of us has to *desire* to create miracles. Although it may seem self-evident now after reading the numerous stories throughout this book, most likely no one ever told you that you were intended to be a miracle and a miracle creator. This newfound discovery then naturally raises this question in your heart: What more can I do to create and expand my miracle-making power?

The first thing to do is to keep yourself plugged into the Source, God. If you wanted to iron a shirt and make it nice and crisp, you would plug in the iron, get it hot, and start ironing immediately. You wouldn't get it hot, unplug it, and then come back a day later expecting to get the wrinkles out, would you? Of course not. That would be a very frustrating experience, and you wouldn't feel very powerful in getting the job done. Yet that's how most people live their lives. They plug into the Source, going to church on Sunday, but then unplugging themselves on Monday morning as they go about their week's activities. And they wonder why they don't experience anything miraculous in them or through them.

If you stayed plugged into your Creator all the time, imagine how often and how powerfully you'd see miracles all around you. It could be a revolutionary idea in your mind right now, but you were endowed with so much potential to be a miracle maker. The desires in your heart are the seed of belief and the beginning of the path to action and future results. God gives you full and complete permission to start receiving and generating miracles for yourself and others. Jesus asked, "Will you never believe in me unless you see miraculous signs and wonders?" (John 4:48 NLT). Do you need to see miraculous signs and wonders, or can you just believe and start to create them?

God is obviously the originator of all miracles past, present, and future—and we read in the Bible that "Jesus is the same yesterday, today, and forever" (Hebrews 13:8 NLT). Through Scripture we also know that "God said, 'Let us make human beings in our image, to be like us'" (Genesis 1:26 NLT). I interpret this to mean, among other things, that we are to make miracles, just as the Father and the Son have done throughout eternity. Don't be overwhelmed by that thought, though. As you remain plugged in and living in a state of wonder, aligning yourself with God's Spirit, miracles big and small will begin to manifest.

So often, we think we need some huge event or idea to make a miracle in our life or someone else's, but we don't. All we need is the strength and conviction to find *one more thing.* What is the *one more thing* you can do to help or serve or encourage someone in need? What is the *one more thing* you can do to change someone's day, or maybe change their life? Today, as you reflect back on all the stories you've read throughout this book, I challenge you to look at your life and the people around you and ask yourself what I call the Miracle Question: *What more can I do?*

The results just may be . . . miraculous.

Twelfth Miracle Scroll

Today I Am a Miracle Maker

Today I am born anew.

I will not let anyone or anything

distract or dissuade me from

believing in my miracles.

I will find and create miracles everywhere.

I will rise to every occasion.

I will welcome miracles happily.

I will accept miracles graciously.

I know the favor of God will pour into my life

every minute and every second of every day.

Conclusion

The Miracle Challenge

As you have read repeatedly throughout this book, I strive to maintain the miracle mindset every day, in every interaction, with everyone I come into contact with. I am always looking for an "in"—some way to step into someone's life and do some small act of grace that takes the course of their day (or maybe their whole life) in a totally new and exciting direction. The "Miracle Question" that we identified in the last chapter is always ringing in my ears: *What more can I do?* That is such a powerful question, and your willingness to make that question a part of your daily life determines whether or not you'll become a miracle maker.

What more can I do? That is such a powerful question, and your willingness to make that question a part of your daily life determines whether or not you'll become a miracle maker.

When Miracles Fail

Of course, we need more than our good intentions to change the world. Remember the words of the apostle Paul: "I can do all things through Christ who strengthens me" (Philippians 4:13 NKJV). I can do all things . . . how? Through the ultimate Miracle Maker. Too often, we get confused about this simple, fundamental principle. We get excited about *our* past successes. We get puffed up about the amazing things we think *we* have done. We start to think that *we* can do anything! But what's the problem with all of those statements? They show a lack of focus, a drifting away from the true source of miracles. We cut the apostle's words short and simply say, "I can do all things—period."

Keeping Your Miracle Perspective

With all of the above in mind, let's go back to where we started. We said early in this book that a miracle is simply God, the Creator of the natural world, intervening and temporarily altering the natural order He established. We discussed "first causes" and "second causes." The first cause is always God. There is no substitute. No matter how many amazing things I witness or how often I get to participate in someone's miracle, I will never be the first cause. That's God's place in the order of things.

However, we also said that God graciously chooses to act through second causes. That's me! That's you! That's where our participation in God's miracles happens. That's the picture of the Master Carpenter (God) choosing the best tool (you or me) for the job at hand. There is no question, for example, that Michelangelo was the driving creative force behind the magnificent statue of David. However, the tools Michelangelo chose for the job were of paramount importance. He no doubt kept his tools in perfect working order, always ready to create something beautiful in his hands. I believe that's exactly how God uses us. Yes, the miracles are ultimately His, but by His grace and goodness, He chooses to do many of those miraculous wonders in and through us!

Taking the Miracle Challenge

If you take nothing else from this book, I pray you remember this: Miracles do not just happen around you; you *are* a miracle! You are God's masterpiece. You were perfectly created for a specific purpose. We saw earlier that God very intentionally crafted every part of your being, and as He did, He knew every good work—every miracle—He would ever call you to perform (Ephesians 2:10).

Miracles do not just happen around you; you *are* a miracle! . . . You were perfectly created for a specific purpose.

You are not an accident, and neither are the millions of daily interactions and opportunities that flow past you in the river of life. God has big things in store for you, and He is constantly bringing miraculous potential right to your feet. Our challenge, as miracle makers, is to step into the flow and take hold of every opportunity that comes our way. So don't just bow down and pray for miracles; keep your head up and your eyes open, and go *be* the miracle in someone's life!

Acknowledgments

WOW! This book is a miracle. The invitation and request to write it was a miracle. Writing it was a miracle. Asking my memory to retrieve and remember the miracles that I have experienced and expressed has been a miracle. My friends' contributions have been miraculous indeed. That it came together so beautifully and fast is an absolute miracle. My dream is that it will open every reader to remember, discover, and find new miracles in their lives. That will cause miracle following miracle.

Ted Squires is a miraculous agent, who came to me to write my opus. What a glorious and delightful request. Ted asked me if I could write a book like my beloved former minister, the late great Dr. Norman Vincent Peal's *The Power of Positive Thinking*. Ted said: "Millions need your book, now more than ever." I could not have heard a more perfected request. I have repetitively thanked him for it. Better yet, Ted has introduced me to the who's who of megachurches, media players, and others who will help me get this book to megamillions of readers.

Byron Williamson the esteemed CEO and president of Worthy Publishing, who at Ted's invitation came out to join Crystal and me over lunch. Together, we decided that I should write a big miracle book that would create miracles in the lives of many, many readers. I am deeply thankful for my editor at Worthy Publishing, Kyle Olund, for going the extra mile and helping to expand the excellence and spirit of my miracle message.

Crystal Dwyer Hansen, my beloved life and marital partner, the wisest and most beautiful woman inside and out who I have ever known, told me to write a chronology of miracles from my life's story. The idea immediately took root and you see the result. This woman inspires me and brings out the absolute best in me. She also keeps me together when occasionally I feel like falling apart, being temporarily overwhelmed. She is my twin flame and ultimate soul mate.

Mitch Sisskind is my editor, friend, and the man who has repetitively helped me "pull the rabbit out of the hat" and assist me in many projects. Mitch knows the soul of my writing. He edits me in my voice and never complains. Mitch simply perfects my work. I am deeply indebted to him. Mitch is a lifelong student of spirituality and wisdom studies. Mitch has edited most of the major writers of our time. I am forever thankful for his wisdom, comprehensiveness, and quiet effectiveness.

My office staff has gone the extra mile on every one of our seven companies while I have been dedicated to writing this in and around world speaking tours, major meetings about my alternative energy company, our new life insurance products, our software company, and other exciting enterprises. Readers assume that writers only write; I have a joyously full life. My thanks to Karen Schoenfeld, our Chief Operating Officer, who has kept everything humming in our absence and smiled through the tumult and chaos, making it look effortless keeping our respective ships afloat. Our thanks to Josh Escamilla, who has grown immensely taking on tasks that he had to master in my stead virtually overnight and did brilliantly well.

And special thanks to all my glorious contributors and friends who really know me, still love me, and appreciate and remember our amazing miracles together.

The Miracle Scrolls

The Miracle Scrolls presented throughout this book have encouraged you to recognize God's amazing work in you and through you. All twelve are included in this section so they're easy to read and meditate on regularly, making you more and more miracle minded each day.

First Miracle Scroll

Miracles Are Natural for Me

God wants my life to be full of miracles.

My life itself is a miracle.

Miracles are happening to me continuously.

I wake daily and experience the miracle of living.

My miracles are expanding and accelerating.

I think about miracles, so they come about.

My dreams are miraculous because

I program myself to them before I sleep,

expecting, thinking, and feeling the joy of miracles.

Upon arising I give myself this affirmation:

Today I expect and happily receive miracles.

Second Miracle Scroll

I Am One of God's Greatest Miracles

I am one of God's greatest miracles.

God made me in His image and likeness (Genesis 1:27).

God created the heavens and the earth.

God created me to create.

I am free to create miracles.

Many of the men and women in the Bible created miracles.

The Source of miracles is the same yesterday,

today, and forever.

Miracles are my inheritance and destiny.

God's destiny for me is to create miracles.

I am and will always be one of God's greatest miracles.

Third Miracle Scroll
I Am Miracle Minded

Miracles are fun to create because I am miracle minded.

I have set my goals to create miracles.

Today and every day I can create exciting miracles.

I have plans to create more and more miracles.

From before my birth God planned on

creating miracles in me and through me.

I am reading this and being reminded

of the promise He made to me

even before I was born.

Fourth Miracle Scroll
I Am a Unique Miracle

I am a unique miracle, unlike any other—ever.

My soul is a miracle.

My mind is a thinking miracle.

My brain is an inventory miracle.

My emotions are a guidance miracle.

My eyes are a miracle. My ears are a miracle.

My hands are a miracle. My mouth is a miracle.

My skin is a miracle. My body is a miracle.

My walking is a miracle. My talking is a miracle.

My thinking is a miracle. My ability to be is a miracle.

My ability to do is a miracle. My ability to have is a miracle.

My ability to serve greatly is a miracle.

My ability to love is a miracle.

Fifth Miracle Scroll
I Expect Miracles

I feel, believe, and expect miracles.

God's promises are the same

yesterday, today, and tomorrow.

God's miracles were fully displayed through

Moses, David, Solomon, and Jesus,

and what God has done for them he will do through me.

My future is miraculous.

I have a miraculous certainty in business and in life.

I am certain that my problems are opportunities in disguise.

I am here to become one of God's greatest miracles.

I was created in God's image, and He is in me.

I feel the breath of God in me now and always.

Sixth Miracle Scroll
I Start Each Day with Love

I will greet this day creating miracles

out of the love in my heart.

My heart is full of love and overflowing

with miracle-making power.

I will use *Love*—

the greatest force in the *Universe*—

to conquer all,

for no hatred can defend itself against *Love*.

Seventh Miracle Scroll
I Am God's Great Masterpiece

I am the love of God made visible.

I was conceived by the love of God

and brought forth to do wonders.

I am rare, and there is value in all rarity;

therefore, I am valuable and

forever increasing my value and worth.

I am a wonderfully unique creature of nature.

I am one of a kind. There is no one else like me.

I am God's masterpiece.

Eighth Miracle Scroll
I Have Unlimited Potential

I have unlimited potential to think, grow, and develop.

Only I can choose what I want to manifest.

My potential hungers for my use.

I can and will vastly increase

my accomplishments a thousandfold

for the benefit of all.

Ninth Miracle Scroll
My Tomorrows Are Extraordinary

The miracle of my birth was a great beginning,

and with God I will extend my miracles daily.

Every day I am passionately on purpose

to do great work, and it excites me to do so.

I will set great and inspiring goals and work

to achieve them.

I will create more and more goals

as destinations for my future achievements.

I will fulfill my potential to its limits.

I will constantly and continually improve my thinking,

language, vocabulary, etiquette, graces, politeness,

and personal skills.

I will be love made visible.

Tenth Miracle Scroll
I Will Survive and Thrive

I will delight in challenges

because I know that with God

I can resolve every crisis.

I will survive and thrive.

Problems are opportunities in disguise.

They are here to inspire my growth

and help me discover creative solutions.

Obstacles before me are there to be overcome.

I will use all my talents and resources to solve them

because I am certain of God's desire

to have me survive and thrive.

Eleventh Miracle Scroll

I Am the Love That Creates Miracles

My heart is full of love,

which is the true miracle-making power.

I can forge love-creating miracles in my mind.

I can create miracles that create more miracles.

Because the secret of secrets is that

miracles are forged by love.

Twelfth Miracle Scroll

Today I Am a Miracle Maker

Today I am born anew.

I will not let anyone or anything

distract or dissuade me from

believing in my miracles.

I will find and create miracles everywhere.

I will rise to every occasion.

I will welcome miracles happily.

I will accept miracles graciously.

I know the favor of God will pour into my life

every minute and every second of every day.

Notes

1. Eric Kuzmiak, "Open-Mic: Greatest Sports Achievements—Do You Believe in Miracles?" (BleacherReport.com, June 11, 2008, accessed February 2, 2015).

2. Rabbi Lawrence Kushner, *God Was in This Place & I, i Did Not Know* (Woodstock, VT: Jewish Lights Publishing, 1991), 25.

3. Barry M. Horstmann, "Billy Graham: A Man with a Mission Impossible," *Cincinnati Post*, June 27, 2002 (http://www.highbeam.com, accessed February 2, 2015).

4. See the story here: http://ilikegiving.com/films/i-like-bike.

About the Author

Mark Victor Hansen is an author and sought-after speaker. He is the cocreator of the Chicken Soup for the Soul book series and brand and has sold more than five hundred million books worldwide. Considered one of the most compelling leaders of our time, Hansen has appeared on television programs such as *Oprah* and the *TODAY* show and in publications such as *Time, USA Today,* and *The New York Times.* He lives in Newport Beach, California.

WORTHY®
PUBLISHING

If you enjoyed this book, will you consider sharing the message with others?

- Mention the book in a Facebook post, Twitter update, Pinterest pin, blog post, or upload a picture through Instagram.

- Recommend this book to those in your small group, book club, workplace, and classes.

- Head over to facebook.com/worthypublishing or facebook.com/MarkVictorHansenFanPage, "LIKE" the page, and post a comment as to what you enjoyed the most.

- Tweet "I recommend reading #MiraclesInYou @MarkVHansen // @worthypub"

- Pick up a copy for someone you know who would be challenged and encouraged by this message.

- Write a book review online.

You can subscribe to Worthy Publishing's newsletter at worthypublishing.com.

WORTHY PUBLISHING
FACEBOOK PAGE

WORTHY PUBLISHING
WEBSITE